FRESS

This book is dedicated to my girls – Madeline, Eleanor, Hannah and Sophie. May you never have to scrabble around trying to piece together ragged old bits of paper with vague instructions on them to cook my food.

An Hachette UK Company
www.hachette.co.uk

First published in Great Britain in 2017 by Mitchell Beazley,
a division of Octopus Publishing Group Ltd, Carmelite House,
50 Victoria Embankment, London EC4Y 0DZ
www.octopusbooks.co.uk

ISBN 978-1-78472-203-6

A CIP catalogue record for this book is available from the British Library.

Printed and bound in China

10 9 8 7 6 5 4 3 2 1

Publisher's Note
The Department of Health advises that eggs should not be consumed
raw. This book contains dishes made with raw or lightly cooked eggs.
It is prudent for more vulnerable people such as pregnant and nursing
mothers, invalids, the elderly, babies and young children to avoid
uncooked or lightly cooked dishes made with eggs. Once prepared
these dishes should be kept refrigerated and used promptly.

Publisher: Alison Starling
Senior Editor: Leanne Bryan
Copy Editor: Jo Richardson
Art Director: Juliette Norsworthy
Designers: Naomi Edmondson and Ella McLean
Photographer: Clare Winfield
Food Stylist: Rosie Reynolds
Props Stylist: Linda Berlin
Illustrator: Ella McLean
Senior Production Manager: Katherine Hockley

FRESS

Def. *(verb)* 'to eat copiously and without restraint'

Bold flavours from a Jewish kitchen

EMMA
SPITZER

Contents

Introduction

I have been cooking since I was eight years old, and never having concentrated much at school, food was the only thing that really held my attention. My mother was not a passionate cook, so I can't claim that my love of cooking was inherited, but she was a good cook and always made sure we had a homemade dinner on the table every night. Most of these dishes were part of the legacy of hearty and homely recipes like stuffed cabbage leaves and pot roast from my Polish grandmother, whom I sadly never met, passed down to her in the customary way of every Jewish mother when her daughter gets married. My mother also drew inspiration from the doyennes of Jewish cuisine of her time such as Evelyn Rose and Florence Greenberg, the results of which included her legendary fried fish balls and rum chocolate mousse.

My cultural heritage is something of a melting pot, with my paternal grandparents coming from Russia in addition to my maternal grandparents hailing from the ghettos of Warsaw, although my parents were both born in the UK. My sisters and I travelled a lot through the Middle East and the Mediterranean as kids and the greatest lasting impression of those cultural expeditions was always the food. I remember sitting in a petrol station at the border between Israel and Lebanon eating warm pitta bread with the best hummus I have ever tasted. It was how people ate out in that part of the country; little kitchens everywhere, from dusty roadside stalls to tiny restaurants in the middle of nowhere, serving dishes that left strong imprints on my memory.

The happiest times in my life have always been associated with the three things I cherish the most: family, food and travel. My family wasn't religious and didn't keep kosher, but we had a strong Jewish identity and food played the biggest part in shaping this. Friday night was the one night of the week that was sacred and the only night we would all eat together as a family. I would come home from school to the waft of roast chicken, the windows all steamy from the pot of golden chicken soup simmering away on the hob. What made the soup that much more special were the particular extras that went into it – the little yellow croutons, the *lokshen* (egg noodles) and tiny golden eggs. Mum would always tell us to watch out for the peppercorns, and as I strain these out of the soup now for my own kids, I wonder why she didn't do the same to spare us the mini incendiary explosions of spice. Then came the fight after the meal to see who could get to the roasting tin first to scrape off all the burnt-on onions, chicken bits and roast potato bottoms.

Food and travel were very much interlinked for me. Establishing a successful career in publishing and advertising in my early 20s wasn't enough to satisfy my aspirations and I fantasized about eating my way around various continents and landscapes. Having been fortunate enough to travel widely as a child, I felt there was more to discover, so I took a year out and embarked on a solo voyage around the world. On return, my eyes wider and my wallet smaller, I paid a visit to Leiths School of Food and Wine to see if I could train as a chef. I had eaten so much amazing and interesting food on my travels, I just wanted to be able to cook as well as I ate. But the diploma course proved too expensive for me, since I had used up all my savings. My ambition was put on hold while I went back to my former career in publishing, although this time I was working for a travel publisher, so it was almost my dream job, as I was paid to travel and stay in some of the world's finest hotels. I ate like a queen.

When I set up my own travel business in 2002, I barely had time to cook and relied upon the vibrant food scene in Camden where I worked and lived. Getting married and having children re-ignited my desire to cook. I am by nature a very ambitious and determined person, so the more I cooked, the better I wanted to be. I secretly always felt that I had a lot to live up to, having a fantastic cook for a mother-in-law; a girl's worst nightmare. My mother-in-law Judith's mother was born in Algeria in North Africa before emigrating to Jerusalem in Israel where she raised Judith along with her eight siblings. Safta, as she was known, which translates as 'grandmother', was a tremendous cook and would regularly host banquets for all the family and their friends. There is much talk around the table to this day of these legendary Moroccan feasts, attended by more people than available table space and chairs. A big couscousière would contain a pot of meat, vegetables and fresh herbs at the bottom, with grains of semolina in the top slowly being steamed in the aromatic vapours from the soup below to make the couscous. There were also spicy fish stews accompanied by side dishes of *mahkuda*, a Moroccan-style tortilla, and *matbucha*, a hot salad of paprika-smothered peppers and tomatoes. They say that Safta stopped living when she had to stop cooking, such was the imperative nature of her gift of effortless hospitality. But the memories of her food live on through Judith as she fondly continues to cook and serve some of her greatest food legacies, and I am extremely proud to be the custodian, in turn, of some of those much-loved and cherished recipes.

I call them recipes in the loosest sense, as they had no formulaic measures or clear written methods, just the notes my mother-in-law made in her head and those I've since written down in a bid to preserve these sacred North African delicacies. Judith deeply regrets not having asked her mother to keep those recipes in a journal, so I hope this book helps to lessen some of that regret when she sees the dishes she worked so hard to recreate in black and white.

In a similar vein, my own recipes for this book have been far harder to write than they have been to cook because I only ever quantify ingredients precisely when I'm baking, so it has been hard to narrow down my normal sausage-finger pinches into teaspoons and contain my freestyle herb-throwing into handfuls. I can only encourage you to be as open-minded in your judgment of what you think will work best for your palate and regard my recipes (baking and anything else technical aside) as approximate guidelines. So feel free to be less heavy-handed with any fiery spices, as I could quite happily scatter raw chillies on almost anything savoury and devour them without hesitation, but appreciate that other people may have a more sensitive reaction to spice.

For the last decade or so, my life has been chaotic to say the least; with four young kids and working full time in the travel business I founded with my sister, you could say that my plate was already pretty full. Entering *MasterChef* took that chaos to a whole new level. I call it my 'life begins' moment, the point at which I was ready to see whether my passion for

cooking was just that or if there was more to discover. I had been a huge fan of the show for many years and always dreamed of sitting at a table with John Torode and Gregg Wallace eating my food. I had no idea that that dream would become a reality or how much it would change my life.

In *MasterChef*, you are asked continually to push the boundaries and the pressure is on every time you cook to produce better results than at the previous stage, so it becomes a gruelling process of experimentation. I lived in my kitchen day and night, trying out different combinations of ingredients and seasonings that drew on both mine and my husband's rich cultural heritage, and my passion for the flavours of the Levant and North Africa. I relished the fact that I was producing dishes that neither John nor Gregg had ever eaten before. You would have thought after all their years of judging that there couldn't be many more surprises in store for them, but having dug deep into my unique culinary treasure trove and translated those precious passed-down dishes into the contemporary culinary language, I wowed them with my unusual flavour combinations.

During this period of intensive activity, if my girls wanted to spend time with me, they had to get involved with me in the kitchen – it was a case of pure selfishness on my part. They ate almost everything I cooked. Being a part of the process meant that they learned so much about food and different flavours, and at the same time it taught me that kids eat much better when they see their meal as a sort of accomplishment. Consequently, I never adapt my dishes for younger palates; as far I'm concerned, kids' food just means a smaller portion and not something different altogether. My recipes are designed to be enjoyed by the whole family, hands big and small digging into sharing plates in the middle of the table. When kids get to help themselves to food, it's amazing what they end up putting on their plates and eating. And using spices doesn't necessarily result in spicy food, just nice warm flavours that sit in the background; if you want spice heat, it can easily be added separately to spare those kids that might be put off by it.

My only objective when I started *MasterChef* was not to go out in the first round, being well aware that I didn't fit the typical *MasterChef* mould. My style of food erred on the generous side, with dishes made to share and rip into at the table – rustic rather than elegant fine dining. I therefore had the added constant task of striving to present my food in a more aesthetically appealing way, mindful that the programme viewers could only see my food, not taste it. So that forced me to think about my cooking in a different way, for which I will forever be thankful.

Reaching the finals of *MasterChef* was beyond my wildest expectations. I managed to impress some of the harshest critics – William Sitwell and Charles Campion to name but two – and this gave me the confidence to really believe myself. Having learned so much during the competition, this was the most important lesson – that confidence is king in the kitchen and a little self-belief can go a long way. John Torode once declared that confident cooks produce confident food, and he wasn't wrong there.

My newfound confidence has resulted in this book where I share with you my favourite recipes from a heritage of which I am fiercely proud, and that I believe every home cook can easily recreate in their own kitchen. We've been so fortunate to have experienced a revival of many Jewish and Middle Eastern classics through the likes of Yotam Ottolenghi and Honey & Co., so this book is not having to break new ground and introduce people to an unfamiliar cuisine. It offers instead an approachable way to prepare these dishes from one home cook to another, my principal aim being to inspire confidence in others in the kitchen and encourage a greater use of spices to pimp up everyday humble ingredients. Above all, I see my food as comfort food – in a good way. It is uncomplicated and (mostly) unfussy, as well as enjoyable to cook!

My family tree

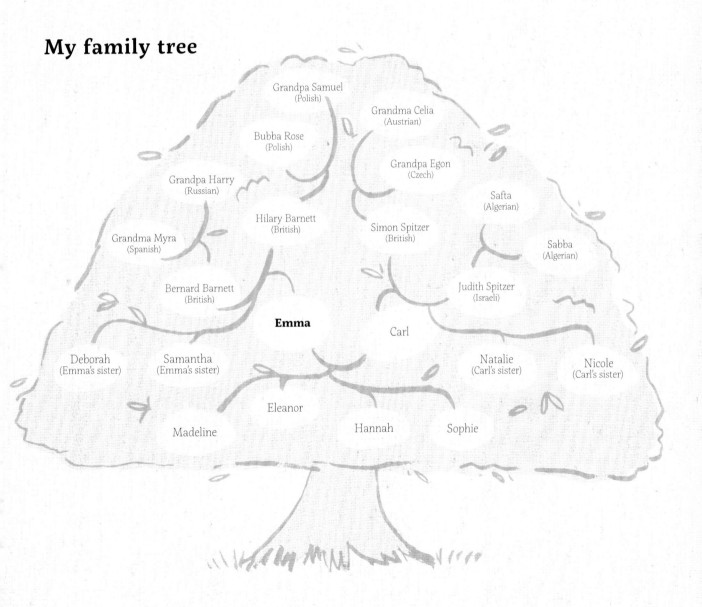

Grandpa Samuel (Polish)

Grandma Celia (Austrian)

Bubba Rose (Polish)

Grandpa Egon (Czech)

Grandpa Harry (Russian)

Safta (Algerian)

Hilary Barnett (British)

Simon Spitzer (British)

Grandma Myra (Spanish)

Sabba (Algerian)

Bernard Barnett (British)

Judith Spitzer (Israeli)

Emma

Carl

Deborah (Emma's sister)

Samantha (Emma's sister)

Natalie (Carl's sister)

Nicole (Carl's sister)

Eleanor

Madeline

Hannah

Sophie

Store-cupboard ingredients

Almost all the ingredients you need for making the recipes in this book are widely available from major supermarkets, specialist grocers or food websites.

The following are some of the most useful food items you will need:

Eggs These are always large unless otherwise specified, and I always use organic free-range.

Fresh herbs Since quantities vary depending on where and how you buy them, it's hard to give specific measurements for herbs; a supermarket packet is around 25g, whereas bunches of herbs from Middle Eastern and Asian grocers or supermarkets weigh in at around 150g. I have therefore generally indicated measures of herbs in handfuls, but you can always use your own judgment. Start with less and add more if you are unsure.

Oils I mostly use rapeseed or corn oil for frying, as it has a higher smoking point. I use olive oil for gentle frying, and a good-quality extra virgin olive oil is essential for dressings and drizzling. However, never use extra virgin for frying because it creates harmful free radicals if heated to a high temperature.

Salt and pepper The king and queen of seasonings. Unless otherwise specified, I use sea salt for a more subtle flavour on dishes such as salads and dips, and as a garnish before serving. Black pepper is always freshly ground from peppercorns and not the pre-packaged ready-ground stuff.

Stocks and stock powders I'm a real heathen when it comes to stock, as I love the powdered variety. Fresh stock has its place and I always made my own when the kids were babies, as I was terrified of the high salt content in shop-bought stocks. Now I simply adjust the amount of additional salt when using powdered stock such as chicken flavour soup and seasoning mix (I like Osem or Thelma) from the kosher section of the supermarket, which I use in every recipe that calls for chicken stock.

Spices

I'm somewhat of a spice junkie – it was a running joke in the *MasterChef* studio that everyone knew which bench was mine from the number of spices on it. My passion stems from visits to exotic markets with my family from a young age and the hours spent walking around taking in all the foreign smells. I have my favourite spices that I just can't manage without, namely cumin, coriander and sumac, but I also love the heady scents of paprika and the earthy tang of za'atar. In fact, I have at least 30 jars of colourful and fragrant concoctions from all over the world stored in my most organized drawer in the house.

Spices can add a real depth of complexity and turn ordinary, everyday dishes into something quite extraordinary, and as many of the recipes throughout the book call for the same spices, I can assure you that your purchases will not end up in what I call the 'spice graveyard' at the back of a cupboard. I would recommend that you invest in some small jars, label them and make them as accessible as possible so that you don't have to remove the contents of your cupboard to find them each time. I have also included alternative spices where there are comparable substitutes in the recipes.

I would always recommend toasting and grinding whole spices in bulk so that you have a constant supply to hand; the flavour is infinitely better and the spices will keep fresh for months in an airtight jar. The best equipment for grinding spices is either a power blender, a coffee grinder or a stick blender. An old-fashioned pestle and mortar will work well too and build some good arm muscle in the process; just sift the spices afterwards to remove any coarse bits.

My top 10 spices

Aleppo pepper (*see* page 44)

baharat (a Middle Eastern spice mix that includes cumin, coriander, cinnamon, paprika, nutmeg, cloves, cardamom and black pepper)

caraway seeds

coriander

cumin

Lebanese 7-spice Mix (*see* page 14)

ras el hanout (a North African mix of many different spices including cardamom, clove, nutmeg, allspice, fennel, cinnamon, coriander, cumin, paprika, black pepper and sometimes dried rosebuds)

smoked paprika

sumac

Za'atar (*see* page 15)

A note on equipment

Since my food is designed to be relatively uncomplicated and easy to cook, no fancy artillery is required other than some simple tools to make the process more pleasurable, and you are likely to have most of the kitchen equipment needed to prepare the recipes. However, where any particular items of kit are required this is mentioned in the recipes.

This lovely warm spice mix, heavy with black pepper and cinnamon, is the perfect partner for all manner of dishes, especially my Chicken Shawarma with Jerusalem and Lebanese Spices (*see* page 76) and Sephardi Rice with Vermicelli and Lentils (*see* page 155). I therefore recommend that you keep a batch permanently in store.

Lebanese 7-spice Mix

Makes 60g

2 tablespoons freshly ground black pepper
2 tablespoons ground allspice
2 tablespoons ground cinnamon
2 teaspoons freshly grated nutmeg
2 teaspoons ground cumin
1 teaspoon ground cloves
1 teaspoon ground ginger

Put all the spices into a bowl and mix together.

Transfer to an airtight container and store in a cool, dark place for up to 6 months.

Tip

If you have a spice grinder or power blender, substitute whole spices for the ready-ground spices. Toast in a dry frying pan over a medium heat until they start to smell fragrant, shaking the pan constantly, then blitz to a coarse powder.

Za'atar is more commonly used throughout the Middle East and the Mediterranean as a table condiment than a spice. It's just as good mixed into a paste with some olive oil for dipping bread into as it is as a crust for meat or fish, or sprinkled over salads. I learned how to make my own version in Jordan and wanted to share this simple recipe so that your store cupboard need never be without it.

Za'atar

Makes 75g

4 tablespoons sesame seeds
8 tablespoons dried thyme (not wild)
1 teaspoon olive oil
2 tablespoons ground sumac
2 tablespoons chickpea flour
¼ teaspoon table salt

Heat a dry frying pan over a medium heat, add the sesame seeds and toast until they are golden brown and starting to smell nutty, shaking the pan constantly. Transfer to a bowl and set aside.

Add the thyme to a spice grinder or power blender and blitz until powder-like in texture. Spread out on a plate. Add the olive oil to the palm of your hand and rub your hands together, then gradually work it into the thyme, just coating it with the oil on your hands.

Stir the thyme into the sesame seeds with the sumac, chickpea flour and salt, making sure that everything is mixed together well.

Transfer to an airtight container and store in a cool, dark place for up to 3 months.

Dukkah translates from the Arabic as 'to pound' and its origin lies in Egypt, where a combination of nuts, herbs and spices are broken down together into a paste or powder and served as a dip with bread, or used as a crust for meat, fish or vegetables. I created my own concoction for my 'calling card' dish on *MasterChef* to crust my rack of lamb. I use this on all manner of dishes, but always serve a bowl of it with some top-quality olive oil with bread as a pre-dinner nibble.

Dukkah

Makes 4 servings

2 tablespoons sesame seeds
50g unsalted pistachio nuts
2 tablespoons ground cumin
2 tablespoons ground coriander
2 teaspoons ground sumac
sea salt
small handful of flat leaf parsley leaves, roughly chopped

Heat a dry frying pan over a medium heat, add the sesame seeds and pistachio nuts and toast for around 5 minutes until lightly golden and fragrant, shaking the pan constantly.

Transfer to a food processor along with the cumin, coriander, sumac, salt to taste and the parsley and pulse until the nuts are finely chopped but still with some texture.

It will keep really well for up to a month if stored in an airtight container in the fridge.

This powerful Tunisian chilli paste is one of the greatest condiments you can have in your fridge. I have experimented with many variations, but this recipe is the one I am happiest with. The sun-dried tomatoes are not a traditional addition to harissa, but I love the flavour they bring as a foil for the strong heat of the chilli. Serve with some olive oil drizzled over the top as a dip for crusty bread, or mix into yogurt, mayonnaise or ketchup to spice them up for use as condiments. Harissa adds a serious depth of flavour to sauces and works really well in marinades too.

Harissa

Makes around a 200ml jar

10 dried red chillies
2 red peppers
1 tablespoon cumin seeds
1 tablespoon coriander seeds
1 teaspoon caraway seeds
2 garlic cloves, peeled and halved
1 teaspoon smoked paprika
1 teaspoon sea salt
2 long red chillies, deseeded and roughly chopped
3 sun-dried tomatoes in oil, drained
1 tablespoon red wine vinegar
115ml rapeseed oil

Soak the dried chillies in hot water for 30 minutes. Drain, then trim off the stalks, deseed and chop roughly – it is advisable to wear gloves for this prep, to protect yourself from the burning effects of the chilli.

Preheat the grill to high. Place the peppers under the grill for around 10–15 minutes, turning once, until the skins have blackened. Transfer to a resealable plastic food bag and seal or to a bowl and immediately cover with clingfilm, then leave for around 20 minutes until cool enough to handle and the skins have loosened. Remove the skins with the back of a knife and discard the stalks and seeds, then roughly chop the flesh.

Heat a dry frying pan over a medium heat, add the cumin, coriander and caraway seeds and toast for 3 minutes, shaking the pan constantly to ensure that they don't burn. Transfer to a pestle and mortar or spice grinder or powder blender (see page 13) and grind to a coarse powder.

Add the garlic cloves with the ground spices, paprika and salt to a food processor and pulse until finely chopped. Add the fresh chillies, dried chillies and sun-dried tomatoes and pulse a few times to combine. Lastly, add the vinegar and oil and blend until you have a coarse paste.

Add to a small (around 200ml) sterilized preserving jar (see page 144), seal and store in the fridge for up to a month.

Small plates for sharing

One of the first High Holidays I spent with my in-laws was Rosh Hashanah, or Jewish New Year. I can clearly remember an extraordinary feast that spread the entire length of two big tables, but it was the bright red bowls of matbucha that really caught my attention. This is the dish that is most often requested by the family because it's pure nostalgia for them, having been made by my husband's grandmother Safta throughout their lives. The head of the family, Safta bore nine children and for many years raised them all by herself. Her legendary cooking is the subject of many family dinners. I can't say whether my matbucha matches up to Safta's, but I can say that it's delicious and the dish that I am most frequently asked to contribute to the table. Matbucha can be eaten with all manner of accompaniments, such as Labneh (see page 47), flatbreads and olives; it's worth making a huge batch and freezing the excess – there is no such thing as too much when it comes to this dish.

Matbucha

Serves 12 as part of a meze spread

6 large red peppers, halved and cores and seeds removed

3 tablespoons olive oil, plus extra for drizzling over the peppers

6 very ripe large (but not beef) tomatoes

3 large garlic cloves, finely chopped

2 large red chillies, deseeded if you want less heat and finely chopped

2 tablespoons sweet paprika

2 teaspoons sea salt

freshly ground black pepper

1–2 pinches of sugar, to taste

Preheat the grill to its highest setting and line a baking tray with foil. Place the peppers, cut-side down, on the tray. Drizzle with olive oil and rub over the skins to ensure that they are well covered. Place under the grill for around 15–20 minutes until they are nicely charred on the top. Remove from the tray, pop into a plastic food bag or a bowl and seal the bag or cover the bowl with clingfilm, then leave for around 20 minutes or until the skins have loosened and they are cool enough to handle.

Meanwhile, score the bottoms of the tomatoes in a crisscross shape and pop into a large bowl. Cover with boiling water and leave for 1 minute. Drain the tomatoes and peel the skins away. Cut the tomatoes in half and scoop the insides out into a bowl for using later. Chop the tomatoes into medium-sized dice and set aside.

Once the peppers are cool, peel the skins away and chop the flesh into strips.

Heat the measured olive oil in a large, heavy-based saucepan, add the garlic and chillies and gently fry for a couple of minutes, taking care not to burn them. Add the peppers and tomatoes and sprinkle over the paprika, then season with the salt and black pepper to taste. Give the mixture a good stir, turn the heat down to a simmer and cook gently for around 2–3 hours, stirring every so often. If you need a bit more liquid, add the reserved tomato insides to a sieve and drain into the pan. If the mixture is reducing too quickly, cover the pan with a lid and continue to simmer over a low heat.

Once the matbucha is the desired consistency, add the sugar to taste and check for seasoning. Remove from the heat and leave to cool. The matbucha can be served hot or cold. It can be stored in an airtight container in the fridge for up to 5 days, or frozen for future use.

On one of my periodical health kicks (usually in January), I decided to make this dip in the way it was intended, that is with natural yogurt and minimal oil, which means it's tasty but virtuous. However, when you add a little more olive oil and some crème fraîche, it's transformed into a really creamy, delicious and indulgent treat. This works really well as a dip or a lovely addition to a meze spread, accompanied by Hummus (*see* page 25) and Challah (*see* page 204). The Israelis make something similar using mayonnaise, so I still consider this to be a marginally healthier option.

Creamy Aubergine Dip

Serves 6

4 good-sized aubergines
table salt, for sprinkling
3 tablespoons olive oil
2 large onions, finely chopped
3 garlic cloves, crushed
2 tablespoons crème fraîche
(or Greek yogurt)
sea salt and freshly ground black pepper

Top and tail the aubergines, then cut into 1cm-thick discs and sprinkle both sides with table salt. Leave for 10 minutes in a colander in the sink to allow some of the bitter juices to drain.

Preheat the grill to a medium-high setting. Rinse the salt from the aubergine slices and pat dry, then brush each side with a tablespoon of the olive oil and season with sea salt and black pepper.

Cook under the grill for around 7 minutes on each side, then remove from the grill and leave until they are cool enough to handle.

Meanwhile, heat the remaining olive oil in a frying pan, add the onions and fry gently for around 10–15 minutes until they are soft and slightly caramelized. Add the garlic and cook for a further 5 minutes.

Remove the skins from the aubergine and finely chop the flesh with a knife – you don't need to be precise here, as it's nice to retain some texture. Add to a bowl with the onions and garlic and crème fraîche (or yogurt) and season to taste with sea salt and black pepper.

This is lovely served at room temperature. It will keep well in an airtight container in the fridge for up to 4 days.

This creamy chickpea dip needs little introduction, so famous is it in its own right, and there are numerous restaurants and street-food outlets as well as large sections of Middle Eastern supermarkets dedicated to showcasing its many different varieties. I may be biased, but I think my father-in-law, aka Bugga, makes the best version of all, and we are lucky enough to enjoy it at almost every family gathering with some warm pitta bread, Challah (*see* page 204) or, my personal favourite, some salted crisps. View the recipe as a blank canvas and feel free to add any kind of topping you fancy to make it even more special; it's all about personal taste, so don't take these quantities too literally.

Hummus

Serves 6–8

2 × 400g cans chickpeas, drained and liquid reserved
juice of 1–2 lemons
2 garlic cloves, crushed, or to taste
1 tablespoon tahini, or to taste
1 teaspoon soy sauce, or to taste
3 tablespoons olive oil, plus a little extra for garnish
1 teaspoon sea salt, or to taste
pinch of ground sumac, to garnish (optional)

Put the chickpeas, reserving 1 tablespoon for garnish, the juice of 1 lemon, the garlic, tahini and soy sauce in a food processor and blend for a few seconds until you have a thick paste.

With the motor running, gradually add the oil and 2 tablespoons of the reserved chickpea liquid. At this point it would be wise to taste the hummus before adding the remaining lemon juice and the salt. Blend for a couple of minutes until you have the right consistency, adding any of the above ingredients as you see fit.

Transfer the mixture to a serving bowl and drizzle over some extra olive oil, then garnish with a pinch of sumac, if you like, and the reserved chickpeas.

It can be stored in an airtight container in the fridge for up to 5 days.

Topping suggestions

* Cut 2 pitta breads into small squares and shallow-fry in vegetable oil in a frying pan until golden brown. Remove and drain on kitchen paper, then place on top of the hummus with a little extra olive oil and some chopped flat leaf parsley.

* Lightly toast a handful of pine nuts in 1 tablespoon of vegetable oil in a frying pan until golden brown. Sprinkle over the top of the hummus with a generous pinch of sweet paprika.

I was fortunate enough to inherit this recipe from a friend of mine, Julian. Over dinner one night, he spoke at length about life growing up on a kibbutz in Israel and how big family banquets using the locally grown ingredients were the mainstay of his childhood. While he discussed all the different dishes his father used to make with great passion, it was this aubergine recipe that clearly ignited the most fire in this voice.

The great thing about this dish is its versatility. It will sit amazingly well on a cold buffet spread, as well as served hot on top of couscous or rice with a dollop of crème fraîche and a nice green salad for a great vegetarian pleaser. Either way, it seems to improve with age, so I would encourage you to make it ahead and leave for a couple of days in the fridge.

Fried Aubergine in Tomato Sauce

Serves 6 as part of a meze spread or 4 as a main

2 large aubergines
6 tablespoons olive oil
2 teaspoons sea salt, or to taste
1 large onion, thinly sliced
2 × 400g cans really good-quality chopped tomatoes
2 tablespoons tomato purée
50ml water
1 tablespoon caster sugar, or to taste
1 tablespoon red wine vinegar
½ teaspoon ground cumin
toasted flatbread, to serve (optional)

Top and tail the aubergines, then slice them into 1cm-thick discs. Heat 2 tablespoons of the oil in a large frying pan over a medium-high heat. Add enough of the aubergine slices to make a single layer, sprinkle over some of the salt and fry gently for around 5–8 minutes or until they are golden brown on both sides. Remove to a plate lined with kitchen paper. Repeat with the remaining aubergine slices, adding a little more of the oil to the pan as needed, and then leave to cool.

While the aubergines are cooling, add the remaining oil to the same pan and fry the onion with a pinch of salt over a medium heat until translucent; this will take around 10 minutes.

Add the canned tomatoes, tomato purée, measured water and sugar to the pan and give the mixture a good stir. Cook over a low heat until the mixture has reduced to a thick consistency, stirring every so often; this will take around 30 minutes, but stay close to the pan so that you can keep an eye on it.

Cut the cooled aubergine slices in half and gently incorporate them into the sauce. Cover the pan with a lid and simmer gently for 10 minutes. Add the vinegar and cumin and mix well, gently breaking down the aubergines to form a thick but not smooth consistency. Taste for seasoning, adding a pinch more salt or sugar if needed.

Remove the pan from the heat and either serve immediately or, even better, leave to cool and serve at room temperature accompanied by toasted flatbread, if liked.

I have a real love and fascination for these little Polish pillows. When my maternal grandparents came to the UK from the ghettos of Warsaw in the 1930s, just like many other immigrants, as Anglophiles they assimilated as best they could into their new life. Where they did stick firmly to their Polish ways, however, was in cooking. My grandmother died before I was born, so I never had the opportunity to try her pierogi first hand and have just had to settle for second-hand instruction. But I have stayed true to her style by making a classic mix of potato and onion, with a few little twists of my own.

Caramelized Onion and Potato Pierogi

Makes around 40–45 pierogi

For the pierogi dough
300g plain flour, plus extra for kneading, if needed, and dusting
½ teaspoon salt
40g unsalted butter, cut into cubes
1 large egg, lightly beaten
75g soured cream

For the filling
40ml vegetable oil
2 large white onions, finely diced
2 white potatoes (about 250g), peeled and chopped into chunks
½ teaspoon sea salt, or to taste
¼ teaspoon ground white pepper, or to taste
3 tablespoons curd cheese

To serve
100g soured cream
1 tablespoon fresh lemon juice

Start by making the dough. If you have a food processor, add all the ingredients to it and pulse until the mixture comes together into a sticky dough. If making by hand, add the flour and salt to a bowl. Using your fingertips, gently work the butter into the flour until the mixture resembles breadcrumbs, then mix in the egg and soured cream to make a dough.

Knead the dough using your fingertips on a floured work surface for 5 minutes, adding a little more flour if it is too sticky. Wrap in clingfilm and leave to rest in the fridge for a minimum of 30 minutes while you prepare the filling.

Heat the oil in a large frying pan, add the onions and gently fry over a very low heat for around 30 minutes until golden brown, stirring often. Drain the onions in a sieve, reserving the oil.

Cook the potatoes in a saucepan of boiling water for 20 minutes, then drain and mash. Mix the mashed potato and onions together and season with the salt and white pepper. Leave the mixture to cool, then add the curd cheese and mix in thoroughly. Check the seasoning.

Roll out the dough on a heavily floured work surface until 2mm thick. Using a 9cm round pastry cutter, cut out circles from the dough, rerolling the trimmings to make more circles.

Place a heaped teaspoonful of the filling in the centre of each circle. Fold over to make a semicircle, then dampen your fingers with water and seal the edges.

Bring a large saucepan of salted water to the boil, drop in the pierogi, in batches, and boil for 5 minutes. Remove with a slotted spoon and drain.

Meanwhile, mix the soured cream and lemon juice together in a bowl ready for serving.

Heat 1 tablespoon of the reserved oil in a large frying pan and fry the pierogi, in batches, for 1–2 minutes on each side until golden brown.

Serve the crispy pierogi hot with the soured cream mixture for dipping.

I spent a long time experimenting with alternative Ashkenazi-style flavours in order to create a unique and tasty pierogi that my grandmother would have been proud of. The combination of salt beef, mustard and dill is a classic one, and works really well when dipped into the accompanying dill and mustard sauce.

Pastrami and Sauerkraut Pierogi with Dill and Mustard Sauce

Makes around 40–45 pierogi

1 quantity Pierogi Dough (*see* opposite)
plain flour, for dusting
vegetable oil, for shallow-frying
salt

For the filling
210g cooled mashed potato
60g pastrami, chopped into small pieces
40g drained sauerkraut
½ cucumber pickle spear, finely chopped
1 teaspoon prepared English mustard
½ teaspoon celery salt
pinch of sea salt, or to taste

For the dill and mustard sauce
3 tablespoons Dijon mustard
1 tablespoon white wine vinegar
100ml rapeseed oil
2 tablespoons finely chopped dill
½ teaspoon sea salt
pinch of ground white pepper (optional)

Mix all the ingredients for the filling together in a large bowl and check for seasoning.

Roll out the pierogi dough on a heavily floured work surface until 2mm thick. Using a 9cm round pastry cutter, cut out circles from the dough, rerolling the trimmings to make more circles.

Place a heaped teaspoonful of the filling in the centre of each circle. Fold over to make a semicircle, then dampen your fingers with water and seal the edges.

Bring a large saucepan of salted water to the boil, drop in the peirogi, in batches, and boil for 5 minutes. Remove with a slotted spoon and drain on a tea towel.

Meanwhile, to make the sauce, mix the mustard and vinegar together in a bowl. Add the oil in a very slow trickle, whisking constantly, until it has all been incorporated, then stir in the remaining ingredients.

Heat 1 tablespoon of oil in a large frying pan and fry the pierogi, in batches, for 1–2 minutes on each side until golden brown.

Serve the crispy pierogi hot with the sauce on the side for dipping.

Tips
* You can miss out the last step of frying and just enjoy the pierogi boiled.
* The pierogi freeze beautifully – just pop them on a tray in a single layer and open freeze them before adding them to a resealable plastic freezer bag.

I first had *kibbeh* in Tel Aviv, Israel, in the Carmel Market, one of the largest food markets in the country, and the second time in a fantastic restaurant called Shoshanna. There are as many variations of this wonderful Middle Eastern dish as there are spellings of it. This is the street-food version; deep-fried and crispy with a lovely warm lamb filling. I view it as a form of cooking therapy when I make these, allowing enough time to try and get the shells really thin and the shape as authentically torpedo-like as possible.

Lamb Kibbeh with Green Tahini

Makes around 20 kibbeh

250g coarse bulgur wheat
1 white onion, roughly chopped
500g minced lamb
1 teaspoon salt
freshly ground black pepper
vegetable oil, for deep-frying
lemon wedges, to serve

For the filling
2 tablespoons olive oil
1 white onion, finely chopped
3 garlic cloves, finely chopped
2 tablespoons pine nuts
500g minced lamb
1 teaspoon Lebanese 7-spice Mix
(*see* page 14)
1 teaspoon ground cumin
1 teaspoon ground coriander
1 teaspoon ground sumac
½ teaspoon ground cinnamon
handful of chopped flat leaf parsley
1 teaspoon sea salt, or to taste
freshly ground black pepper, or to taste

For the green tahini
2 tablespoons tahini
1 garlic clove, crushed
juice of ½ lemon
pinch of sea salt
large handful of finely chopped flat leaf parsley or coriander
freshly ground black pepper

Soak the bulgur in plenty of cold water for at least 30 minutes. Drain and squeeze out the excess water in a tea towel or muslin. Add to a bowl with the onion, lamb, salt and some pepper, and mix together well. Then transfer small amounts of the mixture to your food processor and process until you have smooth, dough-like consistency. Cover and pop in the fridge while you make the filling.

Heat 1 tablespoon of the oil in a frying pan, add the onion and cook gently for around 10 minutes until soft and translucent. Add the garlic and pine nuts and cook for a couple more minutes before adding the lamb, breaking it up with a wooden spoon. Mix all the spices together in a small bowl, then combine with the remaining tablespoon of oil to make a paste. Stir the paste into the meat mixture along with the parsley, add the salt and some pepper and cook until the lamb has just cooked through. At this point, check the seasoning and adjust if necessary. Leave the filling to cool for 15 minutes.

To assemble the kibbeh, take a golf ball-sized amount of the bulgur and meat mixture, roll into a ball and press your middle finger into the centre to make a hole for the filling, turning the ball around a few times on your finger to make the hole deep enough. Place 1–2 teaspoonfuls of the filling in the hole and pinch the top of the ball to seal (wet your hands if the mixture gets too sticky), then reshape into a ball or form into the more traditional torpedo shape. Preheat the oven to 110°C/90°C fan/Gas Mark ¼.

Heat the oil for deep-frying in a deep-fat fryer or a large saucepan (don't fill the pan more than halfway) to around 170°C. Deep-fry the kibbeh, in batches, for around 10 minutes until golden. Remove with a slotted spoon and drain on a plate lined with kitchen paper, then keep the cooked kibbeh warm in the oven while you fry the rest.

Meanwhile, for the green tahini, mix the tahini, garlic and lemon juice to a paste in a bowl. Add some cold water bit by bit to get a runny consistency. Add the salt, parsley or coriander and some black pepper and mix well.

Drizzle the green tahini over the kibbeh, and serve with lemon wedges.

Bourekas were traditionally served in the Middle East on Sabbath mornings after the Jews finished praying in synagogue. Introduced to Israel by Bulgarian immigrants in the late 1940s, today they are typically to be found, stuffed with cheese, on just about every street corner and bakery as the ultimate grab-and-go snack. If you make your own, there are so many possibilities when it comes to choosing a sexy filling. These little parcels are a lovely twist on a traditional sandwich and much lighter too. There are some real flavour bursts going on with this combination of ingredients.

Cumin Potato and Harissa Boureka Sandwich

Makes 4 (or 6) sandwiches

1 sheet of ready-rolled puff pastry
plain flour, for dusting
5 eggs
1 teaspoon nigella seeds
1 teaspoon sesame seeds
1 medium potato, preferably Maris Piper or King Edward, scrubbed
15g butter
1 tablespoon vegetable or rapeseed oil
½ teaspoon sea salt
½ teaspoon ground cumin
1 teaspoon ground coriander
1 teaspoon fresh lemon juice
2 tablespoons Harissa (*see* page 17)
4 tablespoons Tahini Dressing (*see* page 145)
handful of herb leaves, such as coriander, flat leaf parsley and mint

Preheat the oven to 220°C/200°C fan/Gas Mark 7 and line a large baking tray with baking parchment.

Unroll the sheet of pastry on a lightly floured board and cut into rectangles measuring 9 × 13cm. Place on the lined tray. Beat one of the eggs, then brush over the rectangles with a pastry brush. Mix the seeds together in a bowl and sprinkle over each pastry. Bake for 25 minutes or until risen and golden.

Meanwhile, cook the potato whole in a saucepan of boiling water for 10 minutes, then drain and leave to cool slightly.

Cook the remaining 4 eggs in a separate saucepan of boiling water for 7 minutes, then drain and place in a bowl of iced water.

When the potato is cool enough to handle, peel and then slice into 5mm-thick discs. Heat the butter and oil in a large frying pan over a medium-high heat, add the potato slices and sprinkle over the salt, cumin and coriander, then fry for about 4–5 minutes on each side until crisp and golden. Pour over the lemon juice and then transfer the potato slices to a plate.

Shell the eggs and then cut each lengthways into 4 slices.

To assemble the bourekas, cut each rectangle in half horizontally, taking care not to slice all the way through. Spread ½ tablespoon of harissa on the bottom, then top with a layer of potato and egg slices. Pour some of the tahini dressing over the egg, top with some of the herb leaves and eat immediately.

Variation

Try substituting aubergine for the potato. Top and tail a small aubergine, then slice into 5mm-thick discs, sprinkle both sides lightly with table salt and then leave in a colander in the sink to drain for 30 minutes. Rinse the salt from the aubergine slices and pat dry, then fry in 2 tablespoons vegetable oil until golden. Remove and then leave to drain on kitchen paper and cool slightly before using to fill the bourekas.

The form of bourekas varies, as do their fillings – bite-sized for canapés, open sandwiches or made into one large roll and sliced. Grandma Judy makes the best bourekas, simply filled with mature Cheddar and spinach. Using that as my starting point, I have created some fillings of my own. Although a slightly different take on Grandma Judy's more traditional filling, I've earned her seal of approval with my version, as the earthiness of the chard works really well with the cheeses. But feel free to swap the chard for spinach and the cheeses for any of your preferred choices; it's going to be lovely either way when encased in buttery puff pastry.

Chard, Ricotta and Parmesan Bourekas

Makes 15 bourekas

For the filling
200g Swiss chard
table salt
150g ricotta cheese
85g Parmesan cheese
1 egg, beaten
pinch of freshly grated nutmeg
pinch of ground white pepper

For the boureka pastry
1 sheet of ready-rolled puff pastry
plain flour, for dusting
beaten egg, to glaze
2 tablespoons sesame seeds
1 tablespoon nigella seeds

Preheat the oven to 200°C/180°C fan/Gas Mark 6 and line 2 baking trays with baking parchment.

Trim the thick stalks from the Swiss chard and blanch the leaves in a saucepan of salted boiling water for 1–2 minutes. Line a sieve with kitchen paper and then drain the chard, pressing down on the leaves with a wooden spoon to remove all the excess water. Leave to drain and cool, then chop the leaves and combine with the remainder of the filling ingredients.

Unroll the sheet of pastry on a lightly floured work surface and roll out by another 2.5cm all round. Using a 9cm square pastry cutter, cut out squares from the pastry – you should get around 12 from the sheet. Wrap the pastry trimmings in clingfilm and place in the fridge for rerolling to make more squares later.

Place a heaped tablespoonful of the filling in the centre of each square, then brush beaten egg around the border with a pastry brush and fold over to make a triangle. Seal the triangles by pressing down on the edges with the tines of a fork and at the same time making a nice pattern. Place on the lined trays. Reroll and repeat with the chilled pastry trimmings.

Brush each of the triangles liberally with beaten egg (this also helps to prevent the filling from leaking out while baking) and sprinkle over the sesame and nigella seeds.

Bake for 25–30 minutes until puffed up and golden. Enjoy hot or cold.

There is no greater marriage than melted cheese and puff pastry and no greater evidence of how much I love this combination than the fact I've stuffed four different types of cheese into these little parcels. The cheese boureka is a classic that needs little else to make it special but the optional twist of red onion and Za'atar suggested here offers a subtle touch of extra flavour.

Four Cheese Bourekas

Makes 15 bourekas

1 quantity Boureka Pastry (*see* page 36)

For the filling
175g ricotta cheese
85g Parmesan cheese, grated
85g feta cheese, crumbled
85g mature Cheddar, grated
1 egg
pinch of freshly grated nutmeg
pinch of ground white pepper

Optional extras
½ red onion, very finely chopped
2 tablespoons Za'atar (*see* page 15)

Preheat the oven to 200°C/180°C fan/Gas Mark 6 and line 2 baking trays with baking parchment.

Mix all the ingredients for the filling together in a bowl.

Follow the method on page 36 to cut out and fill the boureka pastry with the four cheese filling, adding some of the red onion and a pinch of the za'atar, if using, then bake. Enjoy hot or cold.

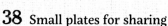

Lox is salmon that has been cured or brined but not smoked, and the dry curing really brings out the flavour of the fish. I was lucky enough to visit New York a few times as a child and to enjoy the typical Jewish delis where lox and cream cheese bagels with pickles were an absolute favourite. Just make sure you purchase a good-quality, thick piece of salmon fillet and remove any bones before starting the curing process.

Lox

Serves 6–8

100g sea salt
150g granulated sugar
1 teaspoon fennel seeds, crushed
grated zest of ½ lemon
70g black peppercorns
1 packet of dill, around 25g
800g piece of skin-on salmon fillet

Mix the salt, sugar, fennel seeds, grated lemon zest and peppercorns together in a bowl.

Add 2 tablespoons of the salt mixture to the base of a non-reactive dish wide enough to hold the salmon and lay 4 or 5 dill sprigs on top. Lightly score the skin of the salmon and then place, skin-side down, on top of the salt mixture and dill. Cover with another 2 tablespoons of the salt mixture or enough to cover. Set the remaining salt mixture aside.

Cover the dish with clingfilm and leave in the fridge overnight.

The next day, drain off any liquid from the salmon, then repeat the process by adding 2 tablespoons of the salt mixture to the base of the dish and another 2 tablespoons on the top of the salmon to cover. Repeat this process over the following 2 days, replenishing the dill sprigs with fresh ones each time.

On the fifth day, rinse the salt mixture from the salmon really thoroughly and dry with kitchen paper. Leave, uncovered, in the fridge overnight to allow the flavours to deepen.

To serve, slice the salmon very thinly from the front of the fillet to the tail and serve on a toasted bagel with lashings of cream cheese. Alternatively, forget the cream cheese and smother with Dill and Mustard Sauce (*see* page 29) instead, along with some capers and red onion.

Falafel is ubiquitous across the Middle East and there are numerous ways to make them, but the humble chickpea is always the staple ingredient. Accompanied with a nice runny Tahini Dressing (*see* page 145), perhaps a dash of chilli sauce and hot chips in doughy warm pitta bread, they are simply heavenly. This is how you will find them served across falafel bars throughout Israel. When you add some succulent white fish as the main ingredient, it lightens them into more of a fishcake texture. They work beautifully with a harissa mayonnaise, perfect for a starter or light supper.

Spiced Cod Falafel with Harissa Mayonnaise

Makes about 20 falafel

200g dried chickpeas, soaked in cold water overnight

table salt

800g skinless cod loin (or any similar white fish fillet, such as coley, hake or haddock), chopped into large pieces

1 onion, quartered

3 garlic cloves, roughly chopped

large handful of coriander, stalks and leaves finely chopped

small handful of dill, stalks and leaves finely chopped

small handful of flat leaf parsley, stalks and leaves finely chopped

2 teaspoons ground cumin

2 teaspoons ground sumac

pinch of cayenne pepper

80g sesame seeds

2 eggs

100g panko breadcrumbs

freshly ground black pepper

sunflower oil, for deep-frying

sea salt flakes

lemon wedges, for squeezing

For the harissa mayonnaise

1 tablespoon Harissa (see page 17)

3–4 tablespoons mayonnaise

Drain the chickpeas, rinse and place in a large saucepan. Cover with plenty of fresh salted water and bring to the boil. Continue to cook for at least 2 hours or until soft, then drain and leave to cool.

Cut the cod into chunks and add to a food processor along with the cooled chickpeas, onion, garlic and herbs. Pulse in short bursts so as not to ruin the delicate nature of the fish – a meat grinder works really well here, if you have one. Transfer to a bowl, add the spices, 1 teaspoon table salt (or 2 teaspoons coarse sea salt), a few twists of black pepper and the sesame seeds and stir through. Cover and pop the mixture into the fridge for 30 minutes.

Wet your hands and roll the mixture into walnut-sized balls. Beat the eggs in a bowl and spread the breadcrumbs out on a plate. Dip each falafel in turn into the beaten egg and then roll in the breadcrumbs.

Preheat the oven to 110°C/90°C fan/Gas Mark ¼.

Heat the oil for deep-frying in a deep-fat fryer or large saucepan to around 150°C (don't fill the pan more than halfway). Deep-fry the falafel, in batches, for about 5–6 minutes until golden. Remove with a slotted spoon and drain on a plate lined with kitchen paper, then keep the cooked falafel warm in the oven while you fry the rest.

Meanwhile, mix the harissa with the mayonnaise, adding more or less of each depending on how hot you want it.

Season the falafel with sea salt flakes and serve immediately accompanied by the harissa mayonnaise and lemon wedges for squeezing over.

Variation

You can leave the coating off completely and just fry the falafel as they are to slightly reduce the calories and time involved.

If I see chicken wings on any menu, I order them, as they are my absolute favourite comfort food, and even better when dunked in a creamy garlicky dressing. Aleppo pepper, named after the town in Syria, is also a personal favourite of mine as a seasoning; used frequently throughout the Middle East, it's now slowly making its way on to supermarket shelves in the West. It offers a relatively low-key chilli heat with a salty undertone, so I've used it generously in this recipe and avoided additional salt. I've worked for some time on this spice mix and cooking method – baking is so much easier (and less calorific) than deep-frying, and the coating has a killer crunch with a warm, spicy heat.

I have my local Turkish restaurant, which keeps my family happy once a week, to thank for the accompanying sauce. We always order the same thing and I ask for extra of their creamy garlic sauce, as I could pretty much eat it with anything. So when I knew I was doing the book, I thought it was high time I gently persuaded them to give me the recipe.

Crispy Baked Chicken Wings with Aleppo Pepper

Makes around 30 wings

1kg chicken wings
1 teaspoon salt
1 teaspoon garlic powder
1 teaspoon lemon pepper
1 teaspoon ground sumac
2 teaspoons Aleppo pepper, plus 1 teaspoon for sprinkling
2 teaspoons smoked paprika
2 teaspoons dried oregano
½ teaspoon English mustard powder
½ teaspoon cayenne pepper
3 teaspoons soft light brown sugar
60g plain flour
80g butter, melted

For the creamy garlic sauce
150g full-fat natural yogurt
1 tablespoon mayonnaise
2 teaspoons olive oil, plus extra if needed
1 garlic clove, crushed
½ teaspoon dried mint
½ teaspoon sea salt, or to taste

Preheat the oven to 220°C/200°C fan/Gas Mark 7. Line a baking tray with a double layer of foil.

Halve the chicken wings at the joint and remove the wing tips, or ask your butcher to do this for you.

Rub the salt into the chicken wings then mix the remaining spices and sugar together in a bowl. Put the flour in a sturdy resealable plastic food bag, add the spice mix and then the chicken wings. Seal the bag and give it a really good shake to ensure that all the wings are well coated.

Place the chicken wings on the lined tray in a single layer and pour the melted butter over each one, turning so that both sides of the wings are covered. Sprinkle with the remaining teaspoon of Aleppo pepper.

Bake for 30 minutes, then turn the wings over and bake for a further 15 minutes until they are crispy and golden and cooked through.

Meanwhile, mix all the ingredients for the creamy garlic sauce together in a bowl and check for seasoning. If it is too thick, thin with a little more olive oil.

Serve the wings hot with the bowl of creamy garlic sauce, or Tahini Dressing (*see* page 145) if you prefer.

This creamy salty dip almost always features at my supper clubs with Matbucha (*see* page 21) and Turkish bread as a sort of rustic amuse bouche; the spiciness of the peppers and tomatoes works really well with the feta. I've also served the two together on a crostini for a canapé. This stands up well too as a lovely dip for some crunchy crudités, or you could serve it with a nice beetroot salad. The possibilities are infinite.

Whipped Feta

Serves 4 generously as part of a meze spread

250g feta cheese
100g Labneh (*see* opposite)
50g crème fraîche
1 teaspoon Dijon mustard
2 teaspoons fresh lemon juice
pinch of ground white pepper

Soak the feta in cold water for around 10 minutes. Drain, crumble into a food processor and blend for a minute or so.

Add the remaining ingredients to the food processor and continue blending until the mixture is smooth, scraping down the sides of the bowl a couple of times to ensure that it is all incorporated.

Transfer the mixture to a bowl, cover and place in the fridge until you are ready to serve. It will keep, refrigerated, for up to around 5 days, but I guarantee it won't last that long!

Labneh is the Middle Eastern equivalent of mayonnaise, and the recipe for it is as simple as its one-word title. Tangy and sharp, this cheese is made from straining yogurt and removing the whey. It's a good job that it's so easy to make, as it's highly addictive.

Labneh

Serves 8

1kg full-fat organic natural yogurt
1 teaspoon sea salt

To serve
good-quality olive oil
1–2 teaspoons Za'atar (*see* page 15)
fresh herbs, such as rosemary, thyme and tarragon (optional)

Mix the yogurt and salt together, then place in a sieve lined with a large piece of muslin. Bring the 4 corners of the cloth together and secure with some string or a clip. Suspend the sieve over a deep bowl with enough between the base of the sieve and bowl to catch all the liquid that drains off the yogurt.

Place in the fridge for a minimum of 6 hours but preferably overnight or up to 48 hours; the longer you leave it to strain, the firmer the labneh will be.

To serve, remove the now-firm labneh from the cloth and place in a bowl. Make a small dip in the top with the back of a spoon and add some good-quality olive oil and sprinkle over the za'atar.

Alternatively, roll the labneh into balls with lightly oiled hands, add to a sterilized preserving jar (*see* page 144) with your favourite fresh herbs and pour over olive oil to cover. Seal the jar and store in the fridge – the labneh will keep for up to 2 weeks.

Variations

* Try adding 1–2 teaspoons ground sumac with the salt at the beginning for a colourful and zingy dip.
* Thin down with fresh lemon juice and add some crushed garlic to make a nice dressing.

This is such a winning combination of flavours and is super easy to prepare. It features on my table at least once a month, usually as a pre-dinner nibble served with some toasted pitta breads.

Artichoke, Spinach and Pistachio Gratin with Pitta Crisps

Serves 6

200g artichoke hearts in oil from a jar, drained and finely chopped

85g cooked spinach, fresh or frozen, finely chopped

85g Parmesan cheese, grated

85g soft white or dried breadcrumbs

2 fat garlic cloves, crushed

50g unsalted pistachio nuts, slightly crushed

125g soured cream or crème fraîche

125g mayonnaise

freshly ground black pepper

For the pitta crisps

3 pitta breads

2 tablespoons olive oil

freshly picked thyme leaves

sea salt

Preheat the oven to 200°C/180°C fan/Gas Mark 6.

Add the artichokes and spinach to a bowl with half the Parmesan, half the breadcrumbs and all the garlic, pistachio nuts, soured cream or crème fraîche and mayonnaise. Give everything a good stir, then season generously with black pepper.

Place the mixture in a small gratin dish and top with the remaining Parmesan and breadcrumbs.

For the pitta crisps, cut the pitta breads into squares and spread out on a baking tray. Brush the olive oil over each square and sprinkle with the thyme leaves and salt.

Bake the gratin for around 20–25 minutes, adding the pitta crisps to the oven for the final 15 minutes, until both the top of the gratin and the pitta crisps are nice and golden. Serve hot or cold.

The closest thing to a good Jewish-style deli in London is The Good Egg in Stoke Newington. While it doesn't do all the classics, it does have one of my favourites, white fish salad, and I am lucky enough to have the recipe. The white fish can be any species of white freshwater fish, which Ashkenazi Jews love to use in cooking (think gefilte fish), that has been smoked. But this may not be easy to get hold of, so unless you are a dab hand at smoking your own, the method below provides an easy and equally tasty alternative.

White Fish Salad

Serves 6 as part of a meze spread

300g coley fillets (or substitute other white fish fillets if unavailable)

½ teaspoon sea salt

1 teaspoon black peppercorns

3 bay leaves

500ml milk

180g cooked smoked trout (smoked haddock will also work well)

6 spring onions, very finely sliced

For the mayonnaise

2 egg yolks

1 tablespoon Dijon mustard

250ml vegetable oil

juice of 1 lemon

½ teaspoon sea salt, if needed

freshly ground black pepper

Put the coley fillets in a non-reactive dish and sprinkle with the sea salt. Cover and leave in the fridge overnight.

The next day, rinse the salt from the coley and pat dry. Place in a saucepan with the peppercorns, bay leaves and milk and simmer gently, uncovered, for 5 minutes. Turn off the heat but leave the coley in the milk for a further 5 minutes. Then transfer the coley to a plate and leave until cool enough to handle.

Meanwhile, make the mayonnaise. Beat the egg yolks and mustard together in a bowl. Add the oil in a very slow trickle, whisking constantly, until it has all been incorporated and the mayonnaise is nice and thick. Beat in half the lemon juice, then season with the salt, if needed, and black pepper to taste.

Flake the coley into a bowl, then add the smoked trout, spring onions and a generous amount of the mayonnaise. If required, add the remaining lemon juice and some more black pepper.

Serve with a toasted bagel and pickles (*see* pages 142–151).

I would roll anything in dukkah, given the opportunity. These little croquettes were created at one of my supper clubs and have become a regular feature on my menus ever since. There is a good amount of heat in them, so you could always pair them with some natural yogurt lightly seasoned with cumin, or tahini if you don't want a spicy dipping sauce.

Dukkah-crusted Lamb Croquettes with Harissa Ketchup

Makes 12–14 croquettes

60g panko breadcrumbs
40g Dukkah (*see* page 16)
50g plain flour
1 egg
sea salt and freshly ground black pepper
vegetable oil, for deep-frying

For the croquettes
2 tablespoons rapeseed or groundnut oil
1 large onion, finely diced
2 garlic cloves, finely chopped
500g minced lamb
2 teaspoons ground cumin
2 teaspoons ground coriander
2 teaspoons Lebanese 7-spice Mix (*see* page 14)
½ teaspoon cayenne pepper
1 teaspoon sea salt

For the harissa ketchup
3 tablespoons tomato ketchup
1 teaspoon Harissa (*see* page 17), or more if you want it hotter
½ teaspoon ground cumin
1 teaspoon fresh lemon juice

For the croquettes, heat the oil in a frying pan, add the onion and gently fry for 10 minutes until lightly golden. Add the garlic and cook for a further 2 minutes, then leave to cool.

Mix the cooled onion and garlic with the lamb and all the remaining croquette ingredients, then shape into small cylinders around 5cm long.

Add the panko and the dukkah to a food processor, if you have one, and pulse a few times to combine and make the crumbs slightly finer. Alternatively, place in a sturdy resealable plastic food bag, seal and crush with a rolling pin. Spread the mixture out on a plate. Season the flour with salt and black pepper and spread out on a separate plate. Beat the egg in a bowl.

Roll the lamb cylinders in the seasoned flour, then dip in the beaten egg mixture and finally coat with the breadcrumb mixture. Leave to chill in the fridge for a minimum of 30 minutes.

Meanwhile, mix all the ingredients for the harissa ketchup together in a bowl and set aside. Preheat the oven to 110°C/90°C fan/Gas Mark ¼.

Heat the oil for deep-frying in a deep-fat fryer or medium saucepan (make sure that the oil is a minimum of 7.5cm deep, but don't fill the pan more than halfway) to around 170°C; check the oil temperature by dropping in a breadcrumb, and when it sizzles, it is ready. Turn the heat down to medium and fry the croquettes, in batches, taking care not to overcrowd the pan, for 5–7 minutes until they are crisp and golden. Remove with a slotted spoon and drain on a plate lined with kitchen paper. Keep the cooked croquettes hot in the oven while you fry the rest.

Serve the croquettes hot, sprinkled with sea salt and with the bowl of harissa ketchup on the side.

Mahkuda is an Algerian dish that my mother-in-law Judith's mother, Safta, would cook up all the time and now my mother-in-law makes during High Holidays. I've taken the same ingredients but constructed it as more of a traditional tortilla-style dish, which works well served either hot or cold, with a crisp salad or some cooked meats. The addition of the cumin and harissa makes it earthy and warming with a gentle kick.

Mahkuda with Harissa

Serves 8

6–7 waxy potatoes

1 large or 2 medium onions, finely diced

300ml olive oil

6 large eggs

2 tablespoons Harissa (*see* page 17), or more if you want it hotter

1 teaspoon ground cumin

sea salt and freshly ground black pepper

Peel the potatoes, then cut in half vertically and slice each half thinly so that you have half-moon shapes; use a mandolin if you have one.

Add the potatoes to a large bowl with the onion, season with salt and mix together to combine.

Heat all but 1 tablespoon of the oil in a nonstick frying pan over a high heat. Check the oil temperature by adding a potato, and if it sizzles, the oil is hot enough. Turn the heat down to medium and add the rest of the potatoes and onion. Cook for 20 minutes in total, turning very carefully in the oil every 5 minutes, or until the potatoes are soft all the way through – you don't want to fry the ingredients too quickly.

Drain the potatoes in a sieve over a bowl, reserving the oil – this has so much flavour, so you absolutely must keep it for other uses.

Beat the eggs in a large bowl, then mix in the harissa and cumin. Season again with salt and some black pepper and then add the potatoes and onion back in. Mix very gently to avoid breaking up the potatoes.

Heat the remaining tablespoon of oil in the same frying pan, add the egg and potato mixture and cook for around 4–5 minutes – you want the heat medium-low here to avoid burning the bottom. Place a plate larger than the diameter of the frying pan over the top and very carefully invert the frying pan to turn the mahkuda over on to the plate. Then return the mahkuda to the pan to cook the other side, adding in any potato that's escaped. Tuck the edges in with a spatula, if need be, to make a nice shape.

Cook for a further 3 minutes and then repeat the turning process as before, placing the plate over the top and inverting the frying pan. The result should be a lovely golden mahkuda. Serve warm.

Tip

Feel free to be creative here and add olives, peppers and any other Mediterranean flavours you feel are appropriate.

There is nothing more comforting than the smell of fried food, except my mum really didn't like the smell of it in the house, so we enjoyed the pleasure of this recipe only once a year on Yom Kippur. She would make the fish balls the day before, partly so that the smell would dissipate before the guests arrived but mainly because traditionally you are meant to have done all your cooking before the 25-hour fast comes in and these are designed to be served cold. I cook these for almost every High Holiday as part of a buffet spread with Egg and Onion (*see* page 62), Chopped Liver (*see* page 63) and Hungarian Cucumber Salad (*see* page 180). Ask your local fishmonger to mince the fish for you in advance – that way you don't have to worry about picking out the bones and processing it yourself.

Fried Fish Balls

Makes about 45 balls

1 large carrot
1 onion
1kg minced white fish
1 egg, beaten
2 tablespoons medium matzo meal
2 teaspoons granulated sugar
½ tablespoon sea salt, or to taste
freshly ground black pepper
2 litres corn oil, for deep-frying

To serve
mayonnaise
lemon wedges

Peel and grate the carrot and onion; use the grating attachment on your food processor if you have one.

Put the minced fish in a large bowl and add the carrot and onion along with the egg, matzo meal, sugar, salt and some black pepper, mixing well with your hands until everything is incorporated.

Heat the oil for deep-frying in a deep-fat fryer or large saucepan (don't fill the pan more than halfway) to around 170°C. Take a small walnut-sized amount of the fish mixture and, using a slotted spoon, drop it carefully into the oil. Cook for 7–8 minutes until it is a deep golden brown. Taste for seasoning and adjust if necessary, then shape the rest of the mixture into ping-pong-sized balls. Fry the fish balls in batches, ensuring that they cook for a minimum of 7 minutes so that the inside is properly cooked. Remove with a slotted spoon and drain on a tray lined with kitchen paper.

Leave to cool completely before serving or, even better, make the day before, then cover and chill until required.

Serve with mayonnaise and lemon wedges, for squeezing over.

Schmear, better known as flavoured cream cheese, is such a lovely, simple spread for toasted bagels or crispy *lavash* crackers. I've classically paired mine with smoked salmon, but added some baked salmon to lighten it a little, along with plenty of fresh lemon juice and dill. Try experimenting with other flavourings of your choice; with a base of rich, creamy cheese, you can't go too far wrong.

Poached and Smoked Salmon Schmear

Serves 6–8

150g piece of salmon fillet
400g full-fat cream cheese
120g smoked salmon, chopped
juice of ½ lemon, or to taste
1 teaspoon sea salt
plenty of freshly ground black pepper
2 tablespoons freshly chopped dill
toasted bagels, to serve

Preheat the oven to 200°C/180°C fan/Gas Mark 6.

Wrap the salmon fillet in foil, place on a baking tray and bake for 8 minutes. The salmon should be almost cooked, but you want it to be a tiny bit pink in the middle. Leave to cool, then remove the skin, if it has some, and check for any stray bones.

Put the cream cheese in a food processor and blend well, scraping down the sides every now and then to ensure that it is all fully blended. Add the smoked salmon, salmon fillet and lemon juice and blend again so that all the ingredients are combined; it is okay to retain some texture in the salmon.

Transfer to a bowl, season with the salt and black pepper and add the chopped dill. Check for seasoning and add more lemon juice if required. Serve with toasted bagels.

One of my favourite Friday night dinners is when we start with Egg and Onion and Chopped Liver (*see* opposite) with Challah (*see* page 204); it never fails to take me back to my childhood. I've offered two variations here, the second a kosher option if eating with a meat meal, replacing the mayonnaise with oil as the binding agent, to make a more traditional recipe in the Jewish diaspora.

Egg and Onion, Two Ways

**Serves 8 as part
of a meze spread**

Way One

10 eggs
4 spring onions, very finely sliced
2 tablespoons good-quality full-fat mayonnaise
sea salt and ground white pepper
a few finely snipped chives, to garnish (optional)

Put the eggs in a saucepan of water and bring to the boil, then turn off the heat and leave for 7 minutes. Drain the eggs, add to cold water and leave until cool enough to handle, then shell.

Place the shelled eggs in a bowl and use a potato masher to chop the eggs as finely as you would like, or use the large holes of a box grater.

Transfer to a serving bowl with the spring onions and mayonnaise, season to taste with salt and white pepper and mix until well combined. Sprinkle with the chives just before serving, if you like.

Tip

For a nice little twist, mix a teaspoon of Dijon mustard into the mayonnaise before adding it to the egg.

Way Two

10 eggs
150ml vegetable oil
3 large white onions, finely diced
½ teaspoon sweet paprika
sea salt and ground white pepper

Cook, shell and grate the eggs as above, then place in a serving bowl.

Heat the oil in a large frying pan, add the onions and gently fry for around 25 minutes until golden brown.

Using a slotted spoon to avoid adding excess oil, spoon the fried onions over the eggs and mix in. Add a little more oil if needed to bind the mixture together. Add the paprika and season to taste with salt and white pepper, then cover and chill in the fridge until ready to serve.

Chopped liver is a very popular starter served on the Sabbath and High Holidays, most typically with a bowl of Egg and Onion next to it (*see* opposite). It's rich and super high in fat and calories, but we forgive it because it tastes so good and everything in moderation, as they say. Traditional recipes call for the use of *schmaltz* (rendered chicken fat) as the binding agent, but vegetable oil is a perfectly acceptable substitute, and besides, I've already strayed quite far from the norm with this twist on a classic.

Chopped Liver

Serves 6 as part of a meze spread

60ml vegetable oil
400g chicken livers
1 large onion, finely diced
80ml Madeira wine
sea salt and freshly ground black pepper
1 hard-boiled egg, shelled and grated (optional)

Heat half the oil in a frying pan over a medium-high heat. Pat the livers dry, and when the oil is hot, add them to the pan and stand back; they will splutter and spit. Turn the heat down slightly and leave the livers to fry, undisturbed, for 3 minutes, then turn and cook for a further 2 minutes before transferring them to a plate.

Heat the remaining oil in the same pan, add the onion and cook for around 10 minutes until it caramelizes a little. Then turn the heat up to its highest setting, throw in the Madeira and leave it cook until it has completely reduced and there is almost no liquid left; this will take no more than 5 minutes.

Drain off any juice collected from the livers and then add them to a food processor with the onion mixture. Season generously with salt and black pepper and blend for a few seconds – you want to retain a bit of texture.

Transfer to a bowl and check for seasoning, then cover and chill in the fridge for a minimum of 6 hours or up to 2 days.

To serve the liver, smear generously on Challah (*see* page 204) or crackers, topped with the grated egg, if you like.

Tip

Prepare this recipe the day before if you have the time, as the flavour will intensify overnight.

Soups

Known as 'Jewish penicillin', this soup is loved by Jews all around the world and there is always a healthy debate about how to cook it best. My mother will forgive me for adapting this slightly. In fact, it was she who recommended I substitute the whole chicken for thighs – they seem to impart so much more flavour, plus the meat remains edible even after the three hours' cooking time. The *kneidlach*, which translates from the Yiddish to 'dumpling', or better known to many as matzah balls, are tasty white fluffy balls that go hand in hand with this soup. You need only patience for this soup; there is very little hard work for an end result that is both comforting and delicious – and, as some would argue, medicinal.

Mummy's Golden Chicken Soup with Kneidlach

Serves 10

8 large chicken thighs, about 900g

4 litres boiling water

2 large onions, unpeeled and halved

6 large carrots, peeled and halved

1 large leek, trimmed, cleaned and chopped

1 small swede, peeled and chopped

2 turnips, peeled and quartered

3 celery sticks, with leaves, chopped

4 tablespoons chicken stock powder or 4 chicken stock cubes

1½ tablespoons sea salt

10 black peppercorns

4 bay leaves

Osem mini croutons, to serve

For the kneidlach (makes 20 balls)

100g medium matzo meal

½ teaspoon table salt, or to taste

¼ teaspoon ground white pepper

1 teaspoon baking powder

¼ teaspoon garlic powder

3 eggs

3 tablespoons vegetable oil

Optional extras

1 tablespoon chicken stock powder or 1 chicken stock cube

1 teaspoon table salt

Put the chicken thighs in a large saucepan and pour over the boiled water. Simmer over a medium heat for a few minutes, allowing the fat to rise to the surface before skimming it off. Then add all the vegetables, the stock powder or cubes, salt, peppercorns and bay leaves. Reduce the heat to a slow simmer and leave the soup to gently bubble away for 3 hours.

In the meantime, make the kneidlach. Mix the matzo meal, salt, white pepper, baking powder and garlic powder together in a bowl. Beat the eggs with the oil, add to the matzo meal mixture and stir through with a fork until just combined. Cover and leave in the fridge for 30 minutes to firm up, or overnight if you are preparing the soup a day ahead.

Remove the chicken from the soup with a slotted spoon, transfer to a bowl and leave to cool slightly. Strain the soup over a large saucepan. Remove the carrots, turnips and swede and set aside; discard the rest of the vegetables. Check for seasoning and add more salt if needed (if you are making ahead, adjust the seasoning when you reheat the soup, as the flavour will intensify).

With damp hands, roll the chilled kneidlach mixture into walnut-sized balls. If cooking the kneidlach in the chicken soup, reheat the soup, and when it is starting to come to the boil, drop in the balls and simmer gently for around 25–30 minutes or until light and fluffy and cooked through. Alternatively, to cook the kneidlach separately, bring a large saucepan of water to boil with the optional extras. Add the matzo balls one by one, cover the pan with the lid and simmer over a low heat for 25–30 minutes until cooked through. Drain and add to a bowl until you are ready to serve the soup.

To serve, pull the skin away from the chicken, and remove the bone with any gristle. Tear the chicken into bite-sized pieces. Cut the reserved veg into bite-sized pieces and place in the base of your soup bowls with some chicken and 2 kneidlach per bowl. Ladle the golden broth over the top and serve sprinkled with mini croutons.

My sister Debbie served this to me as a dinner party starter one night and it was so delicious; even better, it's very healthy. I've recreated it many times since and it works just as well as a filling and virtuous lunch with some lovely dense rye bread or sourdough as it does as a no-fuss dinner party offering. I threw in some leftover cooked chickpeas at the end once and now I always add them – aside from providing some welcome texture to the soup, they also make it into more of a meal in itself.

I would urge you to use really good-quality organic canned cherry tomatoes for this soup and not be tempted to substitute other types of canned tomatoes; only fresh would be an acceptable alternative.

Debbie's Cherry Tomato, Red Lentil and Chickpea Soup

Serves 8

2 white onions
6 carrots
2 celery sticks
3 garlic cloves
olive oil, for sautéeing
250g dried red lentils
3 × 400g cans cherry tomatoes
1.5 litres chicken or vegetable stock
3 bay leaves
a few sprigs of thyme
150g dried chickpeas, soaked and cooked or 400g can chickpeas, drained and rinsed
sea salt and freshly ground black pepper
dollop of crème fraîche (optional)

Peel and finely chop the onions, carrots, celery and garlic, or add to your food processor and pulse until everything is nice and small but not puréed.

Add a few glugs of olive oil to a large saucepan, add the vegetables and sauté over a medium heat for about 10 minutes until they are soft.

Rinse the lentils well until the water runs clear and then add to the saucepan and cook for a minute. Stir in the canned tomatoes and stock and bring to the boil. Add the bay leaves and thyme and season to taste with salt and black pepper. Turn the heat down, pop a lid on and simmer gently for around 35–40 minutes.

When the soup is ready, it will be nice and thick. At this point, you can either blend completely until smooth using a stick blender or by transferring to a blender, or partially blend to keep it thick and chunky.

Add the chickpeas to the soup and continue cooking until they are heated through. Check and adjust the seasoning, then serve with a dollop of crème fraîche if you like.

I absolutely love Jerusalem artichokes – they are so versatile and delicious. The only problem is that the season for them is fairly short, so I tend to find myself making large quantities of soups and purées and stashing them away in the freezer so that I can readily get my fix. The addition of hazelnuts elevates this soup to an ultra-rich and decadent dish, making it a perfect trouble-free starter that can easily be doubled in quantity to feed a small crowd.

Jerusalem Artichoke Soup with Toasted Hazelnuts

Serves 4

2 tablespoons olive oil

25g butter

3 banana shallots, finely chopped

2 celery sticks, finely chopped

1 fat garlic clove, finely chopped

750g Jerusalem artichokes, scrubbed and chopped

1 bay leaf

1 teaspoon wild dried thyme

1 litre hot chicken or vegetable stock

100g blanched hazelnuts

2 tablespoons crème fraîche

juice of ½ lemon

sea salt and freshly ground black pepper

Heat the oil and the butter in a saucepan, add the shallots and celery and cook for a few minutes until they are starting to soften. Add the garlic and continue to cook for a couple more minutes.

Add the Jerusalem artichokes, bay leaf and thyme, season with salt and black pepper and cook for a minute before pouring over the hot stock. Cover the pan with a lid and simmer for 20 minutes until the artichokes are nice and tender.

Heat a dry frying pan over a medium heat, throw in the hazelnuts and toast for around 5 minutes, shaking the pan every so often to ensure that they don't burn. Tip them on to a plate.

Remove the bay leaf from the soup and add about three-quarters of the hazelnuts, chopping the remainder of the nuts and reserving. Blend the soup with a stick blender until smooth, or transfer to a blender to blend. Add the crème fraîche and blend again.

Squeeze the lemon juice over the top, then ladle the soup into bowls and scatter with the reserved chopped hazelnuts.

Pulses and beans are a mainstay of my store cupboard. I grew up eating hearty dishes heavily laden with them and now I too find myself cooking with them frequently. This soup should be nice and thick, and the addition of the turkey rashers makes it a complete meal in a bowl. Serve with a generous amount of crusty bread.

Split Pea and Vegetable Soup

Serves 6

2 tablespoons vegetable or rapeseed oil
150g turkey rashers, thinly sliced
2 onions, finely diced
6 carrots, finely chopped
2 celery sticks, finely chopped
2 garlic cloves, crushed
300g dried green split peas, soaked in cold water overnight
1.5 litres vegetable or chicken stock
2 bay leaves
sea salt and freshly ground black pepper

Heat the oil in a large saucepan, throw in the turkey rashers and fry for a couple of minutes until they start to colour. Add the onions, carrots, celery and garlic and cook over a medium heat for around 5 minutes until the vegetables have softened.

Drain and rinse the split peas, then add to the pan, stirring them into the vegetables, and cover with the stock. Add the bay leaves, some salt (go easy if you are using stock powder) and a few generous twists of black pepper.

Bring the soup to a simmer, then cover with a lid and cook for around 2–2½ hours or until the peas are soft. You may need to add some water to the pan if the soup is too thick.

Pour half the soup out and blend with a stick blender, or transfer to a blender to blend. Return to the rest of the soup, stir to combine and serve.

Big plates with meat & fish

A true *shawarma* consists of heavily spiced meat cooked on a spit, being turned slowly for hours and hours before slivers of the juicy meat are piled high in warm flatbreads with other delicious accompaniments. This is my take on a home-style shawarma, so it's quick and easy to cook yet packed full of flavour. The blend of the peppery cardamom with the warm cinnamon and allspice in the Lebanese spice mix is a marriage made in heaven when it meets a chicken thigh. Try serving this with Sephardi Rice with Vermicelli and Lentils (*see* page 155) and Israeli 'Chik Chak' Salad (*see* page 172), or pile on to some flatbread with chilli sauce.

Chicken Shawarma with Jerusalem and Lebanese Spices

Serves 4

6 boneless, skinless chicken thighs
1 teaspoon ground turmeric
1 teaspoon ground coriander
½ teaspoon ground cardamom
2 heaped teaspoons Lebanese 7-spice Mix (*see* page 14)
2 tablespoons olive oil, plus extra for frying if preferred
sea salt

To serve
grilled flatbreads
Israeli 'Chik Chak' Salad (*see* page 172)
chilli sauce
pickled chillies

Start by laying each chicken thigh in turn between 2 sheets of clingfilm and flattening with a meat mallet or rolling pin until they are roughly an even thickness of around 1cm throughout.

Add the spices to a bowl and stir in the olive oil to make a paste.

Place the chicken in a sturdy resealable plastic food bag with the spice paste and squish it all together until it is well coated. Pop in the fridge for as long as you can to marinate; a minimum of 1 hour, but overnight is preferable.

Heat a nonstick frying pan until smoking; there is enough oil on the chicken not to warrant adding any to the pan, but feel free to if you prefer. Add the chicken to the hot pan and fry over a high heat for about 2 minutes, then turn the heat down to medium and cook for a further 3 minutes or until it has a good deep colour. Turn the chicken over and fry on the other side for another 5 minutes. The thickness of the chicken will determine how long it needs, so use your judgment and check to make sure there is no pink left – there is a fine line between nicely charred and burnt, so keep a close eye on it.

Serve straight away, cut into slices, with grilled flatbreads, chilli sauce and pickled chillies.

The food memories that evoke the strongest feeling of nostalgia are my mum's Friday night roast chicken with onions and really crispy roast potatoes. It was the one night of the week when we all ate together as a family, and it marked the start of the weekend and being able to stay up late (remember *Golden Girls* and *Cheers* anyone?). I would race to the pan before it got washed up to scrape up the burnt-on bits of onion and roast potato, and while you eventually have to deal with the consequences of that degree of crispiness in the washing-up, those delicious morsels are more than worth it. Besides, you are only using one pan. This is such a simple supper with nothing fancy about it, perhaps too simple even to constitute a recipe, but more of a way of celebrating the flavour of one of the most ubiquitous *carne* in the Jewish culinary canon.

Friday Night Chicken with Onions and Roast Potatoes

Serves 6

3 onions, thickly sliced

1 free-range chicken, around 2kg

6 large Maris Piper or King Edward potatoes, peeled and cut into whatever shape you like your roast potatoes to be

3 tablespoons olive oil

1 teaspoon sea salt

freshly ground black pepper

green salad, to serve (optional)

Preheat the oven to 200°C/180°C fan/Gas Mark 6.

Place the onions in your roasting dish – you want one large enough to hold all the potatoes too. Sit the chicken on top, breast-side down, and dot the potatoes all around it. Smear the olive oil generously all over the chicken and the onions and potatoes, and season with the salt and plenty of black pepper.

Roast for 1 hour 45 minutes, turning the potatoes and onions every 25 minutes in the oil and chicken juices. Turn the chicken breast side up to crisp up the skin for the last 30 minutes of the cooking time.

Serve with a green salad, if liked.

Note

Some people prefer to parboil the potatoes first in salted water, but the long cooking time here means that the potatoes cook just as well without this step and turn lovely and crisp.

During *MasterChef*, we were set a brief of choosing someone that inspired us and creating a dish around that person. It was a no-brainer for me; I had to do something with roast chicken, inspired by my mum, but it had to be elevated from the classic bird I knew and loved into a *MasterChef*-worthy creation. This recipe incorporates all my favourite spices. With an hour to cook this dish, I spatchcocked a poussin to allow it to cook faster, but to eliminate the need for any butchery here, I've recreated the recipe using thighs, although it would work with any part of the chicken or, of course, the entire bird. Not only is it very easy to make, it is ridiculously tasty and fit for either a simple family supper or as part of a more elaborate banquet.

Baharat Spiced Chicken

Serves 6

12 bone-in, skin-on chicken thighs

2 red onions, thinly sliced

2 tablespoons baharat

2 teaspoons ground sumac

1 teaspoon ground cumin

1 teaspoon ground coriander

4 preserved lemons, halved and flesh scooped out and discarded

3 garlic cloves, crushed

400ml chicken stock (using 1 tablespoon chicken stock powder)

3 tablespoons olive oil

1 teaspoon sea salt

a few twists of black pepper

rice or couscous, to serve

Add the chicken thighs to a sturdy large resealable plastic food bag with all the other ingredients, then seal well before massaging the bag to mix everything together. Leave to marinate in the fridge for a minimum of 2 hours but preferably overnight.

Preheat the oven to 200°C/180°C fan/Gas Mark 6.

Add the chicken and all the remaining contents of the bag to a baking tray and roast for 45–50 minutes until the chicken is golden brown and the juices run clear when pierced with a knife.

Serve the chicken with a generous amount of the onions and lemon skins over rice or couscous, ladling the juices over the top.

When I found out that I was going to be a contestant on *MasterChef*, I called my husband's cousin Michal in Israel for some help with recipes. She is a very gifted cook with an effortless, down-to-earth style that's reflected in her hospitality. Having been fortunate enough to have sat as a guest at her table, I knew I could trust her. This is an adaptation of her recipe, and while it didn't make the *MasterChef* table for fear of its simplicity, it works beautifully well as a dinner party dish or on a celebration table, in particular for Rosh Hashanah, given its sweet notes and honey.

Sweet Honey Chicken

Serves 6

6 skin-on chicken leg joints or 12 bone-in, skin-on chicken thighs, or a mixture of thighs and drumsticks

12 shallots, peeled but left whole

3 sweet potatoes, scrubbed and cut into wedges

2 bay leaves

5 sprigs of thyme

12 Medjool dates, pitted

sea salt and freshly ground black pepper

rice or couscous, to serve

50g toasted flaked almonds, to garnish

For the sauce

6 tablespoons clear honey

6 tablespoons soy sauce

3 tablespoons balsamic vinegar

2 tablespoons olive oil

2cm piece of fresh root ginger, peeled and grated

3 garlic cloves, crushed

2 cinnamon sticks

1 tablespoon ground coriander

300ml red wine

Preheat the oven to 180°C/160°C fan/Gas Mark 4.

Place the chicken, skin-side up, on a baking tray and arrange the shallots and sweet potato wedges around the chicken.

Mix all the ingredients for the sauce together and pour over the top, ensuring that everything is well covered. Season generously with salt and black pepper, then tuck in the bay leaves and thyme sprigs.

Cover the tray with foil and roast for 30 minutes.

Turn the oven up to 200°C/180°C fan/Gas Mark 6 and remove the foil. Add the dates and give all the ingredients around the chicken a good stir in the sauce, then cook, uncovered, for a further 30 minutes until the chicken is nicely golden and everything has slightly caramelized.

Serve the chicken over a bowl of rice or couscous with lots of the sauce, scattered with the flaked almonds to garnish.

These chicken meatballs really pack a flavour punch. Quick, simple to prepare and healthy, they need nothing more than some plain rice or a fresh salad to accompany them, making for an easy lunch or dinner.

Chicken and Pistachio Meatballs with Coriander Tahini

Serves 6; makes 25 meatballs

For the meatballs
½ onion
100g unsalted pistachio nuts
50g medium matzo meal
handful of tarragon leaves
2 handfuls of coriander, leaves and stalks
2 handfuls of flat leaf parsley, leaves and stalks
1 tablespoon fresh lime juice
2 teaspoons ground cumin
2 teaspoons ground coriander
1 teaspoon chilli flakes
1 teaspoon sea salt
½ teaspoon freshly ground black pepper
500g minced chicken
1 egg, beaten
2 tablespoons olive oil

For the coriander tahini
2 large handfuls of coriander leaves
1 garlic clove, crushed
75g tahini
juice of 1 lemon
pinch of sea salt

To serve
steamed rice
seeds from ½ pomegranate
handful of mint leaves, finely chopped

Add all the meatball ingredients except the chicken, egg and oil to a food processor and pulse until the mixture comes together; you want a coarse, grainy consistency.

Transfer to a large bowl and add the chicken and the egg, working the mixture together with your hands just until it is combined; you don't want to overwork it. Cover and place in the fridge for 30 minutes.

Meanwhile, clean out the food processor, then add all the ingredients for the coriander tahini to it and blend. With the motor running, slowly add some water until you have a loose dressing with the consistency of double cream. Transfer to bowl, cover and refrigerate until needed.

Preheat the oven to 220°C/200°C fan/Gas Mark 7.

Wet your hands and roll the chicken mixture into ping-pong-sized balls. Grease a baking dish large enough to hold the meatballs in a single layer with 1 tablespoon of the olive oil. Brush the remaining tablespoon of oil over the top of the meatballs and bake for 15 minutes.

Serve the meatballs on a bed of steamed rice garnished with the pomegranate seeds and the chopped mint, then drizzle the coriander tahini liberally over the top.

One of the highlights of my trip to Jordan (and there were many) was cooking in the town of Ajloun at the house of Um Hamzeh, a wonderful Palestinian woman who welcomed us graciously into her kitchen. I watched her make this dish, then sat and greedily devoured the result of her hard work – so much flavour from a few simple ingredients. The key is using really good-quality sumac – preferably Turkish, if you can get it – as this is the star of the show. The bread is important too; the large round naan breads they sell in Turkish and Middle Eastern grocers are thick enough to withstand the cooking process. While this recipe looks like a long process, at the end you have a spectacular, showstopping dish for the centre of the table for everyone to tear and share.

'Musakhan' Sumac Chicken

Serves 6–8

12 chicken drumsticks and thighs

2 tablespoons mild curry powder, plus 1 teaspoon

500ml olive oil, plus 3 tablespoons

2 teaspoons sea salt

2 tablespoons pomegranate molasses

3 large onions, finely diced

2 garlic cloves, finely chopped

1 teaspoon freshly ground black pepper

500ml chicken stock

8 tablespoons ground sumac

6 large round naan or taboon breads

To garnish

1 tablespoon olive oil

50g sliced almonds (or use flaked almonds)

Preheat the oven to 200°C/180°C fan/Gas Mark 6. Place the chicken on a baking tray. Mix the 2 tablespoons of curry powder with the 3 tablespoons of olive oil and use a pastry brush to spread over each piece of chicken, then sprinkle with half the salt. Bake the chicken for 35 minutes.

Remove the chicken from the oven and drain the juice into a jug, but leave the chicken in the tray. Brush the pomegranate molasses all over the chicken and return to the oven for a further 20 minutes until the top is golden and crispy and the chicken is cooked through.

While the chicken is cooking, add the onions to a large saucepan with the remaining curry powder, the garlic, black pepper and remaining teaspoon of salt and stir over a high heat, without oil, for 5 minutes. Cover the pan with a lid, turn the heat down to medium and cook for a further 10 minutes, stirring occasionally. Add the remaining 500ml oil, the chicken stock, reserved juices from the chicken pan and 2 tablespoons of the sumac and leave the mixture to boil gently for about 5–7 minutes until the onions are soft.

Cut each bread round into 6 triangles. Using tongs, carefully dunk each triangle into the onion and oil mixture, then place the bread in a single layer in a large, flat, shallow ovenproof paella-style pan. Using a slotted spoon, lift out some onions and spread them over each piece of bread. Then take 2 tablespoons of the remaining sumac and sprinkle it over the top. Bake the bread for 8–10 minutes until it has started to crisp. Repeat the process until you have used up all the bread and have 3 layers. Once all the bread has been baked, top with the chicken pieces and return to the oven for 5 minutes to heat through.

Meanwhile, for the garnish, heat the oil in a frying pan over a medium heat, add the almonds and fry, stirring constantly, until starting to turn golden, then immediately transfer to a plate.

Remove the chicken from the oven and scatter the almonds on top. Serve straight away with plenty of napkins.

The ubiquitous Ashkenazi feel-good food, schnitzel deserves to be on the highest of pedestals. When I went through a typical teenage phase of deciding to be a vegetarian, my mum gave me a week to cave, and when I showed no sign of weakening, she decided to cook schnitzel. Needless to say, the confirmed carnivore I am today can easily be traced back to that one particular mealtime. Bugga, my father-in-law, makes a killer schnitzel, so I have dedicated this recipe to him. Marinating the meat overnight in egg and garlic is not a conventional method, but it really helps to tenderize the meat as well as imparting a lovely flavour. I grew up with the matzo meal crumb, but love the crispier crunch of panko, so I leave the choice up to you.

Bugga's Turkey Schnitzel

Serves 4

4 boneless turkey breast steaks
3 eggs
1 teaspoon sweet paprika
2 garlic cloves, crushed
175g panko breadcrumbs (or substitute 85g medium matzo meal)
sunflower oil, for shallow-frying
sea salt and freshly ground black pepper

To serve
Israeli 'Chik Chak' Salad (optional, *see* page 172)
lemon wedges

Lay each turkey breast steak in turn between 2 sheets of clingfilm and, using a meat mallet or rolling pin, lightly pound the meat until it is around 6mm thick.

Beat the eggs in a large, shallow dish wide enough to hold the turkey steaks in a single layer, then add the paprika and crushed garlic and season generously with salt and black pepper. Lay the turkey steaks in the mixture, turning to coat, cover the dish with clingfilm and leave to marinate in the fridge for at least 2 hours but preferably overnight.

Spread the panko breadcrumbs (or matzo meal) out on a large plate, then coat each turkey steak in turn evenly with the crumbs.

Heat a frying pan with a thin film of oil – you want a depth of around 1cm. Test if the oil is hot enough by dropping in a breadcrumb; when it sizzles, it is ready. Fry the turkey steaks over a medium heat for around 4 minutes on each side until golden brown, turning once.

Remove to a plate lined with kitchen paper or, if not serving straight away, pop on a baking tray lined with foil and place in an oven preheated to 110°C/90°C fan/Gas Mark ¼ to keep warm.

Season the schnitzel with sea salt and serve with Israeli 'Chik Chak' Salad, if liked, and lemon wedges to squeeze over.

This is definitely a special occasion dish and one that I constructed to secure a place in the semi-finals of *MasterChef*. I experimented with lots of different seasonings, but was most proud of my own black za'atar invention, which adds a really interesting flavour to the meat. Take care when scoring the duck skin so that you cut deep enough to render the fat, but not so deep that you penetrate the meat, which can cause it to toughen when cooking.

Seared Duck Breast with a Black Za'atar Crust and Braised Puy Lentils

Serves 2

2 tablespoons black sesame seeds

2 tablespoons fennel seeds

1 teaspoon cumin seeds

2 teaspoons chilli flakes

1 tablespoon ground sumac

½ teaspoon ground cinnamon

1 teaspoon freshly picked thyme leaves

2 duck breasts, preferably Gressingham

2 tablespoons date syrup

sea salt and freshly ground black pepper

For the lentils

250ml chicken or beef stock

2 teaspoons duck fat

1 banana shallot, finely chopped

1 leek, white part only, trimmed, cleaned and finely chopped

2 tablespoons tomato purée

125g dried Puy lentils, rinsed and drained

3 sprigs of thyme

1 garlic clove, peeled but kept whole

2 tablespoons crème fraîche (optional)

sea salt and freshly ground black pepper

Start by making the spiced crust for the duck breast. Heat a dry frying pan over a medium heat, add the black sesame, fennel and cumin seeds and lightly toast, shaking the pan constantly. Crush using a pestle and mortar and then place in a bowl with the remaining spices, thyme and some salt and black pepper.

Pat the duck breasts dry. Using a sharp knife, score the skin in a crisscross pattern. Brush the skin of each of the breasts with the date syrup and then pat about a tablespoonful of the spice mixture on top, rubbing it in to make sure that it is well coated. Place in a dish, cover and leave in the fridge to marinate for up to an hour.

For the lentils, heat the stock in a saucepan. In a separate saucepan, melt the duck fat, add the shallot and leek and cook, stirring, for about 3 minutes until soft. Add the tomato purée and the lentils and cook for a further minute to coat before adding the thyme, garlic and hot stock. Bring to the boil, then reduce to a simmer. Cover the pan and cook, stirring occasionally, for 30–40 minutes until soft but still retaining a bite and the liquid has evaporated; top up with a little hot water if the lentils need more cooking time. Discard the garlic and thyme, season with salt and black pepper and leave to rest in the saucepan, covered, while you cook the duck.

Preheat the oven to 220°C/200°C fan/Gas Mark 7.

Place the duck breasts, skin-side down, in a cold, preferably ovenproof frying pan without any oil over a medium heat for around 6–8 minutes or until the skin is golden brown. Pour off the excess fat and then turn the duck breasts over and cook on the flesh side for a minute to seal. If your pan is ovenproof, transfer to the oven, or transfer the duck breasts to a baking tray, skin-side up, and cook for a further 10 minutes for medium rare, 12 minutes for medium or 15 minutes for well done.

Remove the duck from the oven and leave to rest; it will need a good 5 minutes at least. Meanwhile, add the crème fraîche to the lentils, if using, and stir through. To serve, carve the duck into slices. Place a few spoonfuls of the lentils on the plates and top with the slices of duck.

I have had the pleasure of sharing a sofa with the incredible Claudia Roden on a panel discussing the wonders of Sephardi cuisine. One of the greatest ambassadors of Jewish world cuisine out there today, she has been writing cookbooks for more than 60 years, and her *A Book of Middle Eastern Food*, first published in 1968 and since updated and much enlarged as *The New Book of Middle Eastern Food*, is considered to be the cookery bible among Jews. She kindly gave me permission to feature any recipe from the book of my choosing, and given the many delights to pick from, narrowing down the choice was no straightforward task. In the end I went for her *ghormeh sabzi* because it celebrates my best-loved meat, lamb, with some amazing herbs and spices. It's no wonder that this dish was the favourite of Iranian Jews and remains one of the most popular dishes eaten in Iran today.

Lamb Ghormeh Sabzi

Serves 6

6 tablespoons vegetable oil

1 large onion, finely chopped

1kg boneless lamb shoulder, excess fat trimmed, cut into 2.5cm cubes

1 litre water

3 dried limes

1 teaspoon dried lime powder (or use an extra lime if you can't find it)

2 leeks, green parts included, trimmed, cleaned and chopped

8 spring onions, green parts included, chopped

1 large bunch of flat leaf parsley, chopped

1 small bunch of coriander, chopped

1 small bunch of dill, chopped

1 small bunch of fresh fenugreek leaves, chopped, or 2 tablespoons dried leaves

sea salt and freshly ground black pepper

Heat 2 tablespoons of the oil in a large, heavy-based saucepan, add the onion and fry gently for around 10 minutes until soft. Add the lamb, turning the pieces until they are nicely browned all over. Add the measured water and bring to the boil, skimming any scum that rises to the surface, then turn down the heat. Puncture the dried limes with the tip of a sharp knife and add them to the meat along with the dried lime powder. Season with salt and black pepper.

As soon as you have put the meat in, prepare the green vegetables and herbs. Add the chopped leeks and spring onions to your food processor and pulse until they are very finely chopped.

Heat the remaining oil in a separate large saucepan, add the vegetables and herbs and sauté over a medium heat, stirring often, until they begin to darken. Add to the meat (if you are using dried fenugreek leaves, add these now too) and cook everything together over a low heat, covered, for around 1½–2 hours until the meat is really tender. As the limes soften, squeeze them with the back of a spoon against the side of the pan so that they absorb the liquid and cease to float on the surface.

Serve over plain basmati rice.

Note

Dried limes and lime powder are available from Middle Eastern, Turkish or Asian supermarkets.

Hamin (if you're Sephardi) or *cholent* (if you're Ashkenazi) is one of the only dishes that can actually be called truly Jewish. Jews adopted recipes from the countries in which they settled, often adapting them to kosher dietary laws, so they were in fact interpretations of existing dishes. Hamin is the exception, having been created specifically for Jews observing the rules of the Sabbath when cooking is prohibited. It was prepared on a Friday before the Sabbath started and then kept on a hot plate until after synagogue on the Saturday. This is an assembly job rather than real cooking, as you simply add everything to a slow cooker and leave for 12–15 hours. There is no need to tend the cooker; just let it work its magic. It won't be the most attractive dish you'll ever cook, but it's tasty enough that you can forgive its rather dull brown appearance.

'Hamin' Jewish Stew

Serves 6

1kg potatoes, peeled and halved, or leave whole if they are small

2 large onions, diced

1kg boneless lamb shoulder, excess fat trimmed, cut into 2.5cm cubes

3 marrow bones

1 tablespoon sea salt

½ teaspoon freshly ground black pepper

150g wheat grains or pearl barley, soaked in cold water for 8 hours

150g dried chickpeas, soaked in cold water for 8 hours

6 eggs in their shells, well washed

3 garlic cloves, peeled but left whole

1 litre chicken stock

2 teaspoons sweet paprika

2 teaspoons ground turmeric

2 teaspoons ground cumin

Place the potatoes in the base of a 6–8-litre slow cooker, then sprinkle over the onions and top with the lamb, marrow bones and salt and pepper.

Drain and rinse the wheat or pearly barley and the chickpeas, then add to the cooker with the eggs and garlic cloves.

Heat the chicken stock and mix in the spices, then pour over the contents of the cooker, topping up with water if necessary to ensure that everything is covered.

Cover the cooker pot, set the cooker to low and cook for 12–15 hours.

To serve, shell the eggs and then pile the stew on to plates, adding an egg to each.

Tips

* You could use lamb on the bone instead, provided your slow cooker is big enough to accommodate it.

* If you don't own a slow cooker, use a heavy-based casserole dish and ensure that there is enough water to cover the contents, then leave to cook in an oven preheated to 90°C/70°C fan/Gas Mark ¼ overnight or for 12–14 hours.

I once cooked a lamb shank dish for my family when they came to visit me at my flat share in London. My kitchen was small and poorly equipped, and the oven and hob could be described at best as ropey. Wanting to impress, I spent a fortune on some beautiful shanks, which I lovingly marinated overnight, only to completely destroy them. The oven had packed up just an hour into the three-hour cooking process, so I transferred them to the hob and proceeded to boil them on too high a heat until they took on the texture of shoe leather. Watching my parents and sisters trying to cut (or rather saw) into them was painful to watch when they should have been falling off the bone. They teased me for a long time afterwards whenever the words 'lamb shanks' came up, which is why I was determined to redeem myself. Some 15 years later I decided to revisit the dish in preparation for the finals of *MasterChef* when I tried several different cooking techniques to hit optimum meat-melting consistency. Using the oven is definitely the best option to ensure that the temperature stays even, but I have also cooked this dish in the pressure cooker and it's a close second. So this recipe was born out of my quest for culinary lamb shank redemption, and I can assure you that the meat will fall off the bone, bearing no resemblance to shoe leather.

Lamb Shank Tagine

Serves 4

2 teaspoons ras el hanout
sea salt
50g plain flour
4 French-trimmed lamb shanks
2 tablespoons olive oil
1 onion, finely sliced
1 teaspoon ground cumin
1 teaspoon ground coriander
½ teaspoon ground cardamom
1 teaspoon ground sumac
1 teaspoon ground cinnamon
1 teaspoon dried lime powder
1 teaspoon smoked paprika
1 teaspoon ground turmeric
2 tablespoons tomato purée
1 large tomato, chopped
Continued...

Preheat the oven to 160°C/140°C fan/Gas Mark 3.

Mix the ras el hanout and some salt into the flour, then roll the shanks in the seasoned flour until they are well coated.

Add 1 tablespoon of the oil to a heavy-based casserole dish and brown the shanks all over; do this relatively slowly so that you get a nice caramelization on the lamb without burning the spice. Remove the shanks from the pan to a plate and set aside.

Heat the remaining oil in the pan over a medium heat, add the onion and fry until softened and lightly golden. Add the remaining flour mixture from the shanks to make a roux and fry for a couple of minutes until it is all incorporated. Add all the spices and stir well into the onion mixture, then add the tomato purée and fresh tomato.

Add the shanks back to the pan, turning thoroughly in the onion and spices, then pour the chicken stock over (top up with water if the level of the liquid looks too low; you want the lamb to be almost covered) and add the thyme. Bring the liquid to the boil, pop on the lid and transfer to the oven.

500ml chicken stock
3 sprigs of thyme
6 black garlic cloves
2 teaspoons pomegranate molasses
10 dates, pitted
freshly ground black pepper

To garnish
25g flaked almonds
3 ready-to-eat dried apricots,
thinly sliced
seeds from 1 pomegranate, or a small
tub of ready-prepared seeds
small handful of flat leaf parsley,
finely chopped

Cook for 2 hours, then remove the lid and add the black garlic cloves, pomegranate molasses and dates. Continue cooking for a further 30 minutes, by which time the sauce will have thickened slightly. If you would prefer to reduce it further, remove the lamb shanks to a plate and bring the sauce to a simmer on the hob until it reaches the desired consistency.

Check for seasoning and add a touch of salt if needed and a few twists of black pepper.

Heat a dry pan over a medium heat, add the flaked almonds and toast, moving them around in the pan, until lightly golden.

Transfer the lamb shanks and sauce to a large serving bowl and sprinkle over the apricots, pomegranate seeds, toasted almonds and parsley.

Serve with couscous.

Stuffed cabbage leaves is the dish my mum recalls her mother making the most. Being Polish, it was one of the classics in her repertoire. In parts of Eastern Europe, it's traditional to serve these with a sour tomato and lemon sauce, but I've introduced a Sephardi-style *chraimeh* sauce to the story for an extra flavour dimension and a touch of heat. Some other little additional treats such as barberries and pistachios crept in there too for added texture.

Bubba Rose's Beef and Pistachio Stuffed Cabbage Leaves in Chraimeh Sauce 'Holishkes'

Serves 4; makes around 10–12 rolls

1 large sweetheart cabbage
4 tablespoons Harissa (*see* page 17)

For the chraimeh sauce
3 tablespoons olive oil
3 red peppers
1 onion, roughly diced
6 garlic cloves, sliced
2 red chillies, deseeded and roughly chopped
2 tablespoons smoked paprika
1 tablespoon ground cumin
1 teaspoon ground allspice
3 tablespoons tomato purée
400g can good-quality chopped tomatoes
500ml chicken or vegetable stock
sea salt and freshly ground black pepper

For the stuffing
500g minced beef
200g cooked basmati rice
20g dried barberries
20g unsalted pistachio nuts, roughly chopped
1 teaspoon sea salt
2 teaspoons Lebanese 7-spice Mix (*see* page 14)

Bring a large saucepan of water to the boil. Trim off the bottom of the cabbage, add whole to the boiling water and cook for 3–4 minutes until the leaves have softened and turned slightly transparent. Drain and refresh under cold running water to stop any further cooking, then set aside.

For the sauce, preheat the grill to high. Rub a little of the olive oil over each red pepper and season lightly with salt and black pepper. Place the peppers under the grill for around 10–15 minutes, turning once, until the skins have blackened. Transfer to a resealable plastic food bag or bowl and immediately seal or cover with clingfilm, then leave for around 20 minutes until cool enough to handle and the skins have loosened. Remove the skins with the back of a knife and discard the stalks and seeds, then roughly chop the flesh.

Heat the remaining oil in a wide, flameproof, cast-iron casserole dish, preferably with a lid. Add the onion, garlic and chillies and sauté over a medium heat for 10 minutes until the onions have started to soften. Stir in the spices and cook for a further 5 minutes before adding the peppers, tomato purée, canned tomatoes and stock. Simmer the sauce, uncovered, for 30 minutes, then season with 1 teaspoon salt and black pepper to taste. Transfer the sauce to a blender and blitz until smooth. There is no need to wash the dish at this point, as you will be using it again. Set the sauce aside while you assemble the cabbage.

Add all the stuffing ingredients to a bowl and give everything a good mix.

Peel the outer leaves from the cooled cabbage, taking care not to break them, and lay them on a clean tea towel or some kitchen paper to absorb some of the excess water. You can keep the leaves that are too small to stuff for serving with the dish. Using a small paring knife, carefully shave off some of the thick stalk at the base of each leaf, taking care not to cut through the leaf. Lay out a leaf in front of you with the stalk end closest to you. Add a teaspoon of the harissa and spread it over the leaf. Take around a tablespoonful of the stuffing, roll into a fat sausage shape and place at the

base of the leaf. Fold the base of the leaf over the stuffing and then bring in the sides and roll up. The roll should be compact and the filling secure. Continue this process until you have used all the decent-sized leaves.

Spread a few tablespoonfuls of the sauce on the base of the same dish you used to cook it in. Place the cabbage rolls on top, packing them together as tightly as possible, then pour the remaining sauce over the rolls and bring everything up to a simmer. Cover the dish and cook very gently for an hour. It might be worth checking the liquid halfway through and if necessary add a small amount of boiling water.

When the cooking time is up, using tongs, remove the stuffed cabbage leaves carefully to a serving plate and top with the sauce.

Tips

* You can prepare the stuffing mixture the day before to allow the flavours to develop and make it easier to roll.

* I would highly recommend making a double quantity of the sauce, as it's so versatile that you will want to keep a batch in the freezer.

I became obsessed with beef short ribs ever since eating them for the first time on a trip to New York a few years ago. I now order them whenever they appear on a menu and have spent as much time experimenting with how to cook them best as I have eating them. Short ribs are now widely available at most butchers or can be ordered in advance. Cook these ribs until the meat is clinging to the bones for dear life and have plenty of napkins at the ready; these are super sticky and lip-smackingly good.

Sticky Beef Short Ribs

Serves 6

1 tablespoon rapeseed oil

8 beef short ribs, about 2kg in total, trimmed of any large excess pieces of fat

2 large carrots, peeled and halved

2 celery sticks

2 onions, peeled but left whole

2 star anise

1 cinnamon stick

1.5 litres beef stock

1 tablespoon smoked paprika

3 tablespoons date syrup

1 tablespoon clear honey

sea salt and freshly ground black pepper

Preheat the oven to 180°C/160°C fan/Gas Mark 4.

Heat the oil in a wide, shallow pan over a high heat, and when it is almost smoking, sear the ribs until nicely browned.

Place the short ribs in an even layer in a deep baking tray and season well with salt and pepper. Add the carrots, celery, onions, star anise and cinnamon to the tray, then pour over the beef stock. Cover the tray with foil so that it is well-sealed and cook for 2½–3 hours until the meat is falling off the bone, turning the ribs over twice during the cooking process.

Remove the baking tray from the oven, transfer the ribs to a shallow baking tray lined with foil (which makes for less washing-up) and cover loosely with foil to keep them warm.

Strain the liquid into a saucepan and discard the vegetables and aromatics. Add the smoked paprika, date syrup and honey and bring to the boil. Continue to boil over a high heat for up to 30 minutes or until the mixture is reduced to a thick, syrupy consistency.

Preheat the grill to high. Pour the sauce over each rib, using a basting brush to ensure that all sides are well coated, then flash under the grill for 2–3 minutes until the tops are slightly caramelized.

Transfer the ribs to a plate and serve immediately.

Tip

When I make these for the kids, I shred the meat and serve with the sauce over macaroni or Spaetzle (*see* page 108).

My Aunty Rachel kindly spent one of her precious holiday days when she came over on a visit from Israel cooking with me in my kitchen, and from that I inherited two wonderful dishes, this one and the Hot Red Pepper Fish Stew (*see* page 123). Stuffed artichokes are very popular in Morocco where Rachel's family came from, and there is such a lovely contrast of flavours here in the warm-spiced minced beef and the slightly sharp taste of the artichokes. Most Middle Eastern or Turkish supermarkets stock artichoke bottoms in a jar, but if you can't get those, feel free to use frozen ones, which are widely available, or of course fresh ones when they come into season. Serve with Israeli 'Chik Chak' Salad (*see* page 172).

Aunty Rachel's Beef-stuffed Artichokes

Serves 4

juice of ½ lemon (if using fresh artichokes)

8 artichoke bottoms from a jar, or use frozen if you prefer or fresh when available

2 large eggs

150g plain flour, seasoned with sea salt and freshly ground pepper

4 tablespoons olive oil

For the stuffing

1 small onion, finely diced

250g minced beef

2 teaspoons ground cumin

2 teaspoons baharat

2 teaspoons sweet paprika

½ teaspoon sea salt

½ teaspoon freshly ground black pepper

2 large handfuls of flat leaf parsley, finely chopped

For the sauce

1 tablespoon mushroom or chicken stock powder

½ teaspoon freshly ground black pepper

500ml hot water

Mix all the ingredients for the stuffing together in a bowl, reserving 1 tablespoon of the parsley for garnish. If using fresh artichoke bottoms, rub them with the lemon juice. Stuff each artichoke with 2 tablespoons of the filling, pressing it down well to make it nice and compact.

Beat the eggs in a shallow bowl, and spread the seasoned flour out on a plate. Carefully roll the stuffed artichokes in the beaten egg, then coat in the seasoned flour, dusting off any excess.

Heat the olive oil in a wide, heavy-based frying pan large enough to hold the artichokes in a single layer. When it is hot but not smoking, add the artichokes (in batches if necessary), meat-side down, and fry over a medium heat for 3–4 minutes until the meat is nicely browned on top. Turn them over and fry for a further 3 minutes.

To make the sauce, mix the stock powder and black pepper into the measured hot water until well combined. Put all the artichokes back into the pan, if necessary, and pour over the stock. Simmer, uncovered, for 20 minutes, basting the top of the artichokes every so often, until the sauce has reduced slightly and the artichokes are tender.

Serve the stuffed artichokes immediately, with some of the sauce drizzled over the top, garnished with the reserved parsley.

Tip

The minced beef stuffing can be used for so many other dishes: meatballs, burgers, as a twist on a cottage pie or formed into koftas. I've given quantities to make enough stuffing to fill the number of artichoke bottoms specified, but feel free to double the amounts and use for another dish as suggested.

Some very fond childhood memories stir when I say these two words: salt beef. Trips to Selfridges' salt beef bar were the ultimate reward, a treat to mark some sort of special occasion. I also remember sitting in a diner in New York, Sammy's, that my parents had talked about many a time, where the salt beef on rye sandwich was far taller than the length of my jaw and the pickles were wickedly sharp and crunchy. I had never even thought about making it myself. Rather like filo pastry, why would you make something that's much easier and just as tasty to buy? Well, in the here and now, I am making it myself, and yes, it's a process, and yes, you need to decide that you want to cook it at least a week before you plan to serve it, but it is so unbelievably satisfying, loads more economical and I don't mind admitting how much I love the praise that gets heaped upon me when I serve it with a slightly smug smile.

Salt Beef

Serves around 12 with some left over for later

For the brine
350g coarse sea salt
300g soft light brown sugar
2 teaspoons allspice berries
2 teaspoons juniper berries
2 teaspoons coriander seeds
2 teaspoons black peppercorns
40g Prague powder #1
4 bay leaves
3 cloves
4 litres cold water

For the brisket
3kg piece of flat brisket, fatty if possible
½ garlic bulb, unpeeled
2 celery sticks
1 onion, peeled but left whole
2 carrots, peeled but left whole
3 bay leaves
handful of herbs, such as flat leaf parsley and thyme, or 1 bouquet garni

To serve
mustard
gherkins

Add all the brine seasonings to a very large saucepan and cover with the measured cold water. Bring to the boil and immediately turn off the heat, then leave to cool completely.

When the brine is cool, transfer the brine and brisket to a very large non-reactive container with a lid. Find a weight of some sort to keep the meat submerged in the liquid – a bottle or heavy plate should do the trick – add the lid and then preferably place in the fridge if you can find enough space, or alternatively somewhere else pretty cold. If making in the winter, leaving the container outside would work, provided that it is well sealed. The meat needs to be left to brine for at least 7 days and up to 10, turning it in the liquid once each day.

When you are ready to cook, rinse the brisket really well in cold water. Roll the brisket into a cylinder shape and tie with kitchen string to secure. Place it in a large saucepan with the remaining brisket ingredients, cover with cold water and bring to a very light simmer. Pop the lid on and leave to simmer very gently for around 2–3 hours or until a skewer goes in effortlessly.

Leave the brisket to cool slightly in the water and then lift the lovely wobbly hunk of meat out and carve it into thick generous slices. Serve with mustard and gherkins.

The salt beef will keep for up to a week in the fridge and reheat really well, but just make sure that it's properly sealed in an airtight container.

Note

The Prague powder #1 is integral to achieving that lovely pink colour inside, so please don't omit it; it's available online.

My mum's classic oxtail stew is comfort food at its best and the dish that evokes the greatest amount of nostalgia. It will benefit from being made a day or two ahead of serving, as the flavours deeply intensify the longer they are left to sit. If there are no slurping noises as you suck the juices and goodness from the bones and no licking of fingers around the table as you eat these, then you are most definitely not eating them correctly. *Spaetzle*, pronounced 'shpetzley', are soft egg noodles widely eaten across parts of Northern and Eastern Europe, and are named after their 'little sparrow'-like appearance. My Polish grandmother would make these frequently. I would highly advise investing in a spaetzle maker (inexpensive and easily available online), as you too will want to make these regularly.

Oxtail Stew with Spaetzle

Serves 8

6 tablespoons plain flour

2kg pieces of beef oxtail

3 tablespoons vegetable oil, plus extra if needed

3 large carrots, peeled and cut into chunks

3 celery sticks, chopped

2 onions, diced

1 turnip, peeled and cut into chunks

3 tablespoons tomato purée

500ml beef stock

75cl bottle of red wine

1 bouquet garni

3 bay leaves

sea salt and freshly ground black pepper

For the spaetzle

3 eggs

350ml milk

460g plain flour

½ teaspoon table salt

30g butter

sea salt (if needed) and freshly ground black pepper

Preheat the oven to 150°C/130°C fan/Gas Mark 2.

Spread the flour out on a plate, season generously with salt and black pepper and roll the oxtail pieces in the seasoned flour to coat.

Heat the oil in a heavy-based casserole dish and fry the oxtail pieces quickly in batches over a high heat to colour; don't overcrowd the pan. Remove with a slotted spoon to a plate, keeping some of the juices in the pan.

Add more oil to the pan if needed and then the vegetables. Sauté for a few minutes until they start to soften slightly and take on colour. Stir in the tomato purée and cook for 2 minutes, then add the oxtail back in, cover with the stock and red wine and add the bouquet garni and bay leaves. If the liquid doesn't quite cover the meat, top up with a little more water. Bring to a simmer, then cover with a lid or some foil and place in the oven for around 4–5 hours, stirring every hour or so and making sure there is enough liquid, until the meat is falling off the bone and the sauce is nice and rich.

About 20 minutes before you are ready to serve, bring a saucepan of water to the boil. Make the spaetzle dough by beating the eggs in a large bowl for a few seconds until bubbly. Add the milk and beat to combine. Sift the flour and salt over the top and fold in. The batter will be thick and very elastic but should be loose, so if you need to, add a little more water.

If you don't have a spaetzle maker, add the batter to a piping bag and make a small opening at the end, then squeeze small pieces of the batter out over the pan of boiling water. Alternatively, add the batter to your spaetzle maker and cook as per the instructions. The spaetzle are ready when they have floated to the surface of the water and are nice and fluffy; this will take no more than 2–3 minutes. Transfer to a bowl with a slotted spoon and repeat until you have used up all the batter. Add the butter, some black pepper and sea salt if needed, and mix together.

To serve, divide the spaetzle between plates and top with the oxtail stew.

This dish is a real showstopper and it managed to unanimously unite the guest judges on *MasterChef*, Ping, Luke and Jack (winner and finalists on *MasterChef* 2014), when I cooked it for them. The chickpeas and the Moroccan pesto, better known in North Africa and the Middle East as *chermoula*, are very powerful flavours, but somehow manage to complement rather than overpower the soft and delicate nature of the sea bass. I would normally advocate always using freshly cooked chickpeas, but with the time constraints of the TV programme, I had no choice but to use canned and I think they work just as well in this dish, plus they strip out one extra process.

I practised this dish on family and friends so many times, I think my husband and I must have eaten no less than 15 versions of this dish, but I still love it just as much, especially served with a nice cold glass of Riesling.

Sea Bass over Spiced Chickpeas with Confit Cherry Tomatoes and Moroccan Pesto

Serves 4

4 sea bass fillets
sea salt and freshly ground
black pepper
olive oil, for shallow-frying

For the chickpeas
250g dried chickpeas, soaked in cold water overnight, or 2 × 400g cans chickpeas
2 teaspoons ground coriander
2 teaspoons ground cumin
1 teaspoon caraway seeds
2 teaspoons ground sumac
1 teaspoon freshly ground black pepper
2 teaspoons sweet smoked paprika
½ teaspoon cayenne pepper, or to taste
½ teaspoon sea salt
100ml olive oil
2 garlic cloves, finely chopped
1 tablespoon chopped rosemary leaves
sea salt, if needed

For the Moroccan pesto
6 large handfuls of coriander
Continued...

For the chickpeas, if using dried, drain them of their soaking water, rinse and place in a large saucepan. Cover with plenty of fresh cold water and bring to the boil. Cook for around an hour until soft, then drain and leave to steam dry. If using canned, drain and rinse them really well, then set aside.

To make the pesto, roughly chop the coriander, preserved lemon skins, garlic, ginger and chillies and add to a food processor along with the cumin and some salt and pulse a few times until everything is very finely chopped. Then with the motor running, drizzle the olive oil in slowly until you have a loose pesto-like consistency. Transfer to a bowl, cover and leave in the fridge while you prepare the rest of the dish, to allow the flavours to develop.

For the confit tomatoes, preheat the oven to 120°C/100°C fan/Gas Mark ½. Put the tomatoes on a baking tray lined with foil, add all the other confit ingredients and toss together, ensuring that the tomatoes are well coated with the oil and seasonings. Roast for around 1½ hours or until the tomatoes have slightly dehydrated. Remove from the oven and set aside.

Mix all the spices and salt for the chickpeas together. Heat the oil gently in a deep saucepan large enough to hold the chickpeas, and when the oil is warm (you don't want it hot, otherwise the spices and garlic will burn), add the mixed spices, garlic and rosemary and stir together for a couple of minutes. Then add the chickpeas and cook until everything is nice and hot. Check for seasoning, as this is a good time to add extra cayenne for more of a kick. Remove from the heat and pop on a lid or cover with foil while you cook the fish.

4 preserved lemons, halved and flesh scooped out and discarded
4 garlic cloves, peeled
4cm piece of fresh root ginger, peeled
3 large green chillies, deseeded
1 teaspoon ground cumin
sea salt
6–8 tablespoons olive oil

For the confit cherry tomatoes
12 cherry tomatoes, halved
1 tablespoon olive oil
1 teaspoon sea salt
1 teaspoon granulated sugar
1 garlic clove, crushed
freshly ground black pepper

Run your fingers down the flesh side of the sea bass fillets to make sure that all the bones have been removed (a pair of tweezers are handy for removing them if necessary), and if desired, trim the bottom and top of the fillets on the diagonal to make for a neater presentation. Season the sea bass fillets on both sides with salt and black pepper. Heat a large frying pan, or 2 if you can't fit the fish into one, over a high heat and add a tablespoon of olive oil. When it is smoking, add the fish, skin-side down, and press down gently on the flesh with a spatula to stop it curling. Take care at this point, as the oil will splutter a bit. Turn the heat down very slightly and leave the fish to cook, undisturbed, for 3 minutes. You can tell when the fish is almost cooked by checking the translucency. Turn the fish over carefully and cook on the other side for 1 minute, or a maximum of 2 minutes if they are particularly large fillets.

Transfer the fish, flesh-side down, to a plate to rest while you assemble the rest of the dish.

Give the pesto a stir and add a bit more olive oil if needed. Place a few heaped tablespoonfuls of the chickpeas on the plate, 6 cherry tomato halves around the chickpeas and then top with the sea bass, skin-side up, adding a line of pesto over the fish and a drizzle around the plate.

Tip

I prefer to use whole spices where possible for the chickpea seasoning. Toast the coriander and cumin seeds in large quantities in a dry frying pan over a medium heat until fragrant, shaking the pan constantly, then grind them with a spice grinder or power blender so that you always have this mix to hand. It's great with other pulses such as cannellini and borlotti beans, or a lovely addition for pimping up a basic tomato sauce.

I have loved using dukkah ever since I discovered it on my travels in Egypt. I use it like a pesto on almost anything, and when I first tried it on a simple piece of white fish, I knew it was a recipe I had to share. The crunch against the soft white flesh of the fish gives a lovely texture combination and it's one of those dishes that requires very little effort for an impressive result. Feel free to substitute any other meaty white fish such as hake or halibut for the cod; it even works well with salmon. The dish needs few accompaniments other than some buttered green beans or a fresh green salad.

Cod Loin with a Dukkah Crust

Serves 4

4 cod loins
½ teaspoon sea salt
freshly ground black pepper

For the crumb
1 quantity Dukkah (*see* page 16)
2 tablespoons olive oil

Preheat the oven to 180°C/160°C fan/Gas Mark 4.

For the crumb, tip the dukkah into a shallow bowl and slowly drizzle in the olive oil until the mixture is nice and moist.

Place the cod loins on a baking tray, season with the salt and some black pepper and spread the crumb evenly and generously over the top of each piece.

Bake for 10–12 minutes, depending on the thickness of the loins, until the crust is golden and the fish is cooked through.

My dad used to make this a lot for us; it was one of the few dishes he could make by himself. Its simplicity is what makes it so special – maximum flavour from minimal effort. The sesame oil and almonds work so well together with the earthiness of the trout. I would recommend removing the heads of the fish before serving to anyone who may have a squeamish disposition.

Pan-fried Trout with Sesame and Almonds

Serves 2

1 tablespoon olive oil
2 whole trout, gutted and scaled
1 tablespoon toasted sesame oil
50g flaked almonds
sea salt and freshly ground black pepper

To serve
buttered new potatoes
green beans
crisp green salad

Start by heating the olive oil in a large frying pan over a medium-high heat until nice and hot.

Season the trout with salt and black pepper and add to the pan. Turn the heat down to medium and fry for 5 minutes on one side.

Turn the fish over and add the sesame oil and flaked almonds, then cook for a further 5 minutes.

Serve immediately with buttered new potatoes and green beans or a crisp green salad.

This salmon recipe is so easy and is equally good served hot with plain boiled rice and green beans, or at room temperature with my Buckwheat and Barberry Salad (*see* page 188). It takes very little time to prepare, and dotted with some little pomegranate gems, it looks delightful on the plate. You can also serve this to kids; the sweetness of the pomegranate is an instant winner.

Sticky Pomegranate Salmon

Serves 4

2 teaspoons soft dark brown sugar
1 teaspoon ground sumac
1 teaspoon cornflour
½ teaspoon sea salt
4 skin-on salmon fillets
freshly ground black pepper
1 tablespoon vegetable or groundnut oil
1 tablespoon pomegranate molasses
Buckwheat and Barberry Salad with Spiced Pomegranate Dressing (*see* page 188), to serve
seeds from ½ pomegranate, to garnish

Preheat the oven to 200°C/180°C fan/Gas Mark 6.

Mix the sugar, sumac, cornflour and salt together, then rub over the flesh side of the salmon fillets and add a twist of black pepper over the top.

Heat an ovenproof frying pan over a high heat and add the oil. When it is very hot, add the salmon fillets, flesh-side down, and reduce the heat to medium. Sear for 2 minutes, then turn the fillets over and cook on the skin side for a further minute. Using a pastry brush, spread the pomegranate molasses evenly over each fillet.

Transfer the pan to the oven and cook for a further 8–10 minutes.

If you don't have an ovenproof frying pan, transfer the salmon to a baking tray lined with foil before placing in the oven.

Serve the salmon at room temperature on a bed of buckwheat and barberry salad and garnished with pomegranate seeds.

I like to involve my kids in the preparation of these, as their little hands make surprisingly neat little cakes. This works really well as a starter served on a bed of the Fennel, Orange and Carrot Salad (*see* page 187) or as a lovely family dinner. The fishcakes benefit from being made a little in advance and chilled so that they hold together better when fried.

Salmon and Sweet Potato Fishcakes with Lime Za'atar Yogurt

Serves 4 as a main or 6 as a starter; makes around 14 fishcakes

3 tablespoons olive oil
2 sweet potatoes, around 500g in total, scrubbed
4 skinless salmon fillets (or remove skin), about 650g in total
1 small bunch of dill
8 black peppercorns
1 small bunch of coriander leaves, finely chopped
juice of 1 lemon
3 tablespoons plain flour
2 eggs, beaten
250g medium matzo meal
sea salt and freshly ground black pepper

For the lime za'atar yogurt
500g natural yogurt
1 tablespoon Za'atar (*see* page 15)
grated zest and juice of 2 limes

Preheat the oven to 200°C/180°C fan/Gas Mark 6.

Rub 1 tablespoon of the oil into the sweet potatoes and season with salt and black pepper, then pop them on a baking tray and roast for around 40 minutes–1 hour, depending on their size, until cooked all the way through. Leave to cool while you make the fishcakes.

Place the salmon fillets in a wide, shallow pan with the dill and peppercorns, and barely cover with water. Gently poach, uncovered, for 8–10 minutes until just cooked through. Lift the salmon from the poaching water and flake into a large bowl.

Halve the sweet potatoes, scoop out the flesh and add to the fish along with the coriander and lemon juice. Season well with salt and black pepper and mix together thoroughly. If you have the time, cover and chill the mixture in the fridge for 30 minutes to make the cakes easier to form. Shape the mixture into palm-sized cakes.

Put the flour, eggs and matzo meal in 3 separate shallow bowls. Season the flour with salt and black pepper, then coat the cakes in the seasoned flour, dip into the beaten egg and then roll in the matzo meal. Repeat the egg and matzo meal coating for a second time if you want an extra-crispy fishcake.

Place the fishcakes on a tray lined with baking parchment or foil and refrigerate until you are ready to fry.

Mix the ingredients for the lime za'atar yogurt together in a bowl, then cover and refrigerate until you are ready to serve.

Heat the remaining 2 tablespoons of oil in a wide frying pan and fry the fishcakes, in batches, over a medium heat for around 3 minutes on each side until they are nicely golden.

Serve with a generous spoon of the yogurt on the side and a crisp salad.

Tip

If you can't find matzo meal, you can substitute any other breadcrumbs of your choice; panko would be my next favourite.

I made a version of this recipe on *MasterChef* to achieve a place in the final line-up of three contestants. The guest judge happened to be the guru of fish, Nathan Outlaw, and the dish was very much given the thumbs-up. I served it with spiced meat-stuffed Turkish manti (like tiny ravioli) and some fancy garnishes, but it was the sauce that was the star of the show and overshadowed all the other elements on the plate. I have pared my recipe back to make cooking this special occasion dish much simpler and used meaty monkfish, which stands up well to the robust flavours in the sauce.

Moroccan Spiced Monkfish with Fennel, Leek and Cream Sauce

Serves 4

2 tablespoons olive oil

3 teaspoons ras el hanout

2 thick pieces of monkish fillet, around 350g each

1 large fennel bulb, woody stalk and core removed and fronds reserved to garnish, very thinly sliced (preferably with a mandolin if you have one)

1 large leek, white part only, trimmed, cleaned and finely diced

2 garlic cloves, finely chopped

½ teaspoon ground turmeric

2 tablespoons white wine

500ml vegetable stock

200ml double cream

1 heaped teaspoon Dijon mustard

½ teaspoon sea salt

freshly ground black pepper

To serve
steamed fine green beans, drizzled with oil and lemon juice
buttered steamed new potatoes

Mix 1 tablespoon of the oil with 1 heaped teaspoon of the ras el hanout in a small bowl to make a loose paste. Spread over the monkfish fillets in a dish using a pastry brush, cover and leave to marinate in the fridge for an hour.

Preheat the oven to 200°C/180°C fan/Gas Mark 6.

Heat the remaining tablespoon of oil in a large, deep frying pan over a high heat, and when it is smoking, add the monkfish and sear quickly until it is golden brown on all sides.

Transfer the monkfish to a baking tray and roast for 10–12 minutes until it is cooked through. Remove from the oven and leave to rest for a few minutes under some tented foil.

While the monkfish is roasting, throw into the same frying pan you used to sear the fish the fennel, leek, garlic, remaining ras el hanout and turmeric. Stir together for a couple of minutes before deglazing the pan with the white wine. Leave the wine to cook out for a minute, stirring constantly, then add the stock. Turn the heat down very slightly and leave the sauce to bubble away and reduce for 10 minutes or until its reduced by two-thirds. Add the cream and the mustard and keep stirring for a further 3 minutes. Season with the salt and black pepper to taste.

Divide the sauce between 4 shallow bowls or plates. Slice the monkish into generous rounds and place neatly on top of the sauce in the centre. Serve immediately, sprinkled with the reserved fennel fronds, with some fine green beans drizzled with oil and lemon juice and a bowl of buttered new potatoes on the side.

I am so lucky to have married into an extended family of outstanding cooks. My husband's Aunty Rachel is one of those women who makes cooking look effortless. She glides around her kitchen in Israel, and more recently my kitchen when she came to help, working so fast that I couldn't keep up with my pen and pad. I kept handing her spoons in the hope that she would at least give me some calculated measurements, but her instinct, like many confident cooks, was just to throw in a pinch of this and a drizzle of this, working only by sight and taste. I have constructed this recipe as best I can, but would ask with this one, like many others of mine, that you use your own judgment when it comes to the spicy seasoning. It has some heat yet not enough to detract from the delicate fish. But feel free to be more heavy-handed with the Aleppo pepper if you prefer, or if you are substituting hot paprika for the Aleppo pepper, try adding a pinch of cayenne pepper too.

Hot Red Pepper Fish Stew

Serves 4

1 large red pepper, cored, deseeded and cut into thin rings

2 large ripe tomatoes, cut into medium-thick slices

1 green chilli, seeds included, roughly diced

75ml rapeseed oil

1 teaspoon sea salt

½ teaspoon freshly ground black pepper

1 tablespoon Aleppo pepper or pul biber/Turkish red pepper flakes (or substitute hot paprika if you can't find either)

2 teaspoons sweet smoked paprika

125ml water

4 skinless haddock or cod loins, around 150g each

juice of ½ lemon

2 large handfuls of coriander leaves, roughly chopped

3 garlic cloves, finely sliced

boiled rice or crusty bread, to serve

Lay the pepper rings on the base of a wide, shallow, ovenproof saucepan, then layer the tomatoes over the top. Sprinkle over the chilli.

Mix the oil, half the salt, the black pepper, Aleppo pepper and paprika together. Pour over the vegetables, then top up with the measured water and bring to a simmer. Cover with a lid and cook over a low heat for 30 minutes.

Add the fish pieces on top of the vegetables, squeeze over the lemon juice and sprinkle with the remaining ½ teaspoon of salt, then scatter over the coriander and garlic. Replace the lid and simmer for a further 15 minutes, spooning the liquid over the fish every few minutes.

Meanwhile, preheat the oven to 190°C/170°C fan/Gas Mark 5.

Remove the lid from the pan and transfer it to the oven to cook for a further 20 minutes.

Serve with simple boiled rice or some crusty bread.

Big plates with veg

Freekeh, whose ancient origins lie in the Middle East and North African regions, is made from green, unripe wheat and has become known as an alternative grain to couscous and rice. Its robust and nutty flavour lends itself perfectly to a risotto where it can stand up really well to strong spices. I cooked a freekeh risotto similar to this one on *MasterChef*, which I served with chicken and courgettes, but I have promoted it to centre stage here, as it needs little else in the way of accompaniments.

Freekeh Risotto with Roasted Cashews and Minted Soured Cream

Serves 4

2 tablespoons olive or rapeseed oil
1 onion, finely chopped
3 garlic cloves, finely chopped
1 teaspoon ground cinnamon
1 teaspoon ground allspice
2 teaspoons ras el hanout
250g freekeh, rinsed
500ml vegetable or chicken stock, plus extra if needed
100g raw cashew nuts
grated zest of 1 lemon
large handful of flat leaf parsley, finely chopped
150g Parmesan cheese, grated

For the minted soured cream
300ml soured cream
2 garlic cloves, crushed
1 tablespoon finely chopped mint
juice of ½ lemon, or to taste
sea salt and freshly ground black pepper

Heat the oil in a medium saucepan, add the onion and garlic and gently sauté for around 10 minutes until softened. Add the spices and cook, stirring, for a couple of minutes, then add the freekeh and stock.

Cook, uncovered, over a low heat for around 30–40 minutes until the freekeh is cooked through but still has a little bite. You may need to add a bit more stock if the liquid has been absorbed before the freekeh is ready.

Meanwhile, preheat the oven to 200°C/180°C fan/Gas Mark 6. Spread the cashew nuts out on a baking tray and roast for 10 minutes until golden. Leave to cool, then roughly chop; you want them left as large as possible.

Once the freekeh is cooked, remove the pan from the heat and stir in the lemon zest along with all but a handful of the cashews, parsley and Parmesan.

Mix all the ingredients for the minted soured cream together in a bowl and season to taste with salt and black pepper.

Ladle the risotto into shallow bowls, then sprinkle with the reserved cashews, parsley and Parmesan, top with some of the minted soured cream and serve.

Tip

Any leftover risotto can be shaped into little walnut-sized balls with dampened hands, then rolled in seasoned flour, beaten egg and panko breadcrumbs and deep-fried until golden brown.

I acquired this recipe some years ago after extracting it from a hotel chef in Cyprus. This style of couscous is typical across the Mediterranean, with so much flavour from so few ingredients, and works beautifully with my Chicken Shawarma with Jerusalem and Lebanese Spices (*see* page 76) or Cod Loin with a Dukkah Crust (*see* page 113). My kids are very happy with a bowl of this and nothing more than some grated cheese on top. I've kept the butter optional, as it's not strictly necessary, but it does add a lovely creamy flavour.

Mediterranean Couscous

Serves 4

2 tablespoons olive oil

1 small onion, chopped

30g dried vermicelli noodles, broken into small pieces

400g can chopped tomatoes

1 vegetable stock cube

200g coarse bulgur wheat

25g unsalted butter (optional)

sea salt and freshly ground black pepper

Heat the olive oil in a medium saucepan, add the onion and fry over a medium heat until soft. Add the vermicelli and cook, stirring, with the onion until lightly golden.

Pour the canned tomatoes into the pan, then add the stock cube to the empty tomato can, pour in boiling water to fill the can about halfway and stir to dissolve the cube.

Add the stock to the saucepan, bring the contents of the pan up to the boil and add the bulgur wheat. Give it all a good stir to ensure that the bulgur is well incorporated into the tomatoes and then add the butter, if using.

Switch off the heat, cover the pan with a lid and leave the mixture to sit for around 20–25 minutes until the bulgur has cooked through. If it needs a little longer, just pop the lid back on so that it can continue to steam. Once ready, fork through the grains and season generously with salt and black pepper.

Risotto is the ultimate comfort food. In my quest to find ways of simplifying the process while extracting the most flavour, this fragrant and creamy dish was born and it now features regularly at my supper clubs as a popular vegetarian main. Only the occasional stir is required; far lower maintenance than a traditional risotto and less cooking time too.

Preserved Lemon Orzo and Butternut Squash Risotto with Sugar Snap Peas

Serves 6

3 tablespoons olive oil

1 small white onion, finely chopped

2 garlic cloves, finely chopped

1 small butternut squash, peeled, deseeded and grated

250g orzo pasta

650ml vegetable stock

2 small preserved lemons or 1 large, halved and pips removed

40g butter

40g Parmesan cheese, grated

125g sugar snap peas

1 teaspoon fresh lemon juice

1 teaspoon ground sumac

sea salt and freshly ground black pepper

Heat 2 tablespoons of the oil in a saucepan, add the onion and cook gently for 5 minutes, then add the garlic and continue cooking until the onion is soft and translucent. Add the butternut squash and cook for 5 minutes, then add the orzo, stirring well to incorporate.

Pour over the stock, turn the heat down to a simmer and pop the lid on. Cook gently for around 10–15 minutes, stirring every so often so that the pasta doesn't stick.

While the risotto is cooking, blitz the preserved lemons in a blender, skin and all, to a paste and set aside.

The risotto is cooked when the orzo is nice and soft. Turn off the heat and add the preserved lemon paste, butter and Parmesan, and season well with salt and black pepper. Give it all a good stir through and then leave the lid on while you prepare the sugar snap peas.

Heat the remaining tablespoon of oil in a wok over a high heat, and when it is smoking, throw in the sugar snaps and stand back, as they will splutter and spit. Toss them in the wok for around a minute or so until they have charred slightly; you don't want to overcook them, as they should still be crunchy. Add a pinch of salt, the lemon juice and sumac and give a final shake to the pan.

Spoon a generous amount of risotto into shallow soup bowls or plates and then top with the sugar snaps and a final twist of black pepper.

Tip

For fussy kids, just leave out the preserved lemon paste, as it has quite a distinctive flavour that they may find a bit overpowering.

This dish makes a lovely and robust vegetarian main. The warm spice from the ras el hanout paired with the braised fennel and soft chickpeas is a pleasing combination, and while there are a few processes involved to achieve the end result, it can all be prepared ahead and served at room temperature.

Moroccan Stuffed Sweet Potato with Braised Fennel and Tahini

Serves 4

2 large or 3 medium sweet potatoes, scrubbed

2 tablespoons olive oil

sea salt

green salad or Israeli 'Chik Chak' Salad (see page 172), to serve

For the stuffing

2 fennel bulbs

50g butter

200ml vegetable or chicken stock

50g mung beans, soaked in cold water overnight

1 onion, finely diced

2 fat garlic cloves, finely chopped

400g can chickpeas

1 teaspoon ras el hanout

½ teaspoon sea salt

2 large handfuls of coriander, finely chopped

For the spiced date dressing

3 tablespoons extra virgin olive oil

1 tablespoon date syrup

2 teaspoons white balsamic vinegar

1 teaspoon ras el hanout

pinch of sea salt

twist of black pepper

For the tahini dressing

3 tablespoons tahini

1 tablespoon natural yogurt

juice of ½ lemon

pinch of sea salt

Preheat the oven to 200°C/180°C fan/Gas Mark 6.

Cut the sweet potatoes in half lengthways and place, cut-side down, on a baking tray. Rub a little of the olive oil over the skins and sprinkle lightly with sea salt. Bake in the oven for 40–45 minutes until tender.

For the stuffing, cut the woody stalks off the fennel bulbs, then cut the bulbs in half lengthways. Melt the butter in a frying pan over a medium-high heat, and when it starts to foam, add the fennel, cut-side down. Reduce the heat to medium and cook the fennel for 15 minutes, turning every so often until both sides are golden. When the fennel has started to caramelize, add the stock and bring to the boil. Cover and cook for a further 5 minutes. Uncover and continue to cook for another 5 minutes until the stock has almost evaporated and the fennel is nearly cooked through but still retains some bite.

Drain and rinse the mung beans, then put in a saucepan and cover with plenty of cold water. Bring to the boil and boil for around 15 minutes until the beans are cooked through but not soft.

Meanwhile, heat the remaining olive oil in a pan, add the onion and gently fry for 10 minutes until soft. Add the garlic and cook for a further 5 minutes. Drain and rinse the chickpeas, then add to the pan with the ras el hanout and salt. Cook until the chickpeas are coated in the spiced onions and warmed through. Drain the mung beans, then stir into the chickpea mixture and continue to cook for a couple of minutes. Transfer to a large bowl. Chop the braised fennel into bite-sized pieces and add to the bowl.

Whisk the ingredients for the spiced date dressing together in a small bowl.

In a separate bowl, mix the ingredients for the tahini dressing together, then add a little cold water while stirring until you achieve a pouring consistency.

To assemble, pour the spiced date dressing over the stuffing mixture, then add the coriander and stir through. Transfer each sweet potato half to a plate, flesh-side up and make a deep cut down the centre to create a hole for the stuffing. Spoon a generous amount of the stuffing into each potato half, then drizzle the tahini dressing liberally over the top. Serve the dish with any remaining tahini in a bowl on the side and accompanied by a green salad or Israeli 'Chik Chak' Salad.

Aubergines are so meaty and their sponge-like flesh makes them a great vegetable to stuff. There is texture to this dish as well as great flavour, and it can also be made ahead of time; just add the crumb before reheating and serving.

Tomato-stuffed Aubergine with a Sourdough and Walnut Crumb

Serves 4

2 large aubergines
1 teaspoon table salt
2 slices of sourdough bread
5 tablespoons olive oil
2 teaspoons Za'atar (*see* page 15)
50g walnut halves
1 tablespoon fresh thyme leaves or 1 teaspoon dried thyme
1 large red onion, thinly sliced
1 teaspoon red wine vinegar
2 teaspoons soft dark brown sugar
3 garlic cloves, finely chopped
1 teaspoon ground cumin
½ teaspoon ground cinnamon
1 teaspoon sweet paprika
400g can chopped tomatoes
½ teaspoon granulated sugar
200ml vegetable stock
sea salt and freshly ground black pepper
a few fresh oregano leaves or a pinch of dried oregano, to garnish (optional)

Preheat the oven to 180°C/160°C fan/Gas Mark 4.

Halve the aubergines lengthways and carefully scoop out the flesh, making sure that you leave around a 2mm layer of flesh in the skins. Reserve the flesh in a bowl for using later. Lightly sprinkle the table salt over the aubergine skins and leave in the fridge for 30 minutes.

Roughly cube the sourdough and then toss with 1 tablespoon of the olive oil and the za'atar. Spread out on a baking tray and bake for 20 minutes until they have fully dried out. Add the walnuts to the tray and bake together for a further 10 minutes.

Transfer the sourdough and walnuts to a food processor, add the thyme and pulse until the bread and nuts are a coarse rubble consistency.

Start the sauce by adding 2 tablespoons of the olive oil to a saucepan and frying the aubergine flesh over a high heat until it is golden. Remove from the pan and set aside. Place the same pan back on the heat and turn the heat down to low. Add another tablespoon of oil and gently fry the onion until it is soft and translucent, then add the vinegar and brown sugar and cook, stirring, for a further 5 minutes until the onion starts to caramelize slightly. Add the garlic and spices and cook for 2 minutes before adding the canned tomatoes, aubergine flesh, granulated sugar and sea salt to taste. Simmer gently, uncovered, for 10 minutes.

While the sauce is simmering, rinse the salt from aubergine skins and pat dry gently with a tea towel. Add the remaining tablespoon of oil to a frying pan and fry the skins over a medium heat for 5 minutes on each side (make sure you are wearing an apron for this stage, as they are likely to splutter and spit).

Remove the aubergines to a deep-sided roasting dish or baking tray; you want them to fit snugly side by side. Check the seasoning of the tomato sauce, then spoon generously into the skins. Grind some black pepper over the top and pour the stock into the pan around the aubergines. Cover with foil and bake for 20 minutes, then remove the foil, add the sourdough crumb and bake for a further 10 minutes.

Serve with a garnish of fresh oregano leaves or a pinch of dried, if liked.

Amba is a commonly used spice throughout Israel. It has a tangy, sharp and slightly spicy flavour that can really enhance a humble everyday vegetable like a courgette. I would happily offer a substitute spice if there was one, but the uniqueness of this dish lies in its really distinctive flavour. You can find amba, also known as mango or amchoor/amchur powder, at most Middle Eastern or Indian supermarkets, or failing that, buy it online. Feel free, however, to use raisins instead of the barberries if you can't find them. This dish goes well with other small plates, such as Caramelized Butternut Squash with Whipped Feta and Zhoug (*see* page 178), Fried Aubergine in Tomato Sauce (*see* page 26) and even Sticky Pomegranate Salmon (*see* page 117).

Amba-spiced Courgettes with Barberries and Labneh

Serves 4

2 tablespoons olive oil

1 white onion, finely diced

2 courgettes, halved lengthways and sliced

1 teaspoon amba spice (mango or amchoor/amchur powder)

juice of 1 lemon

pinch of salt, if needed

3 heaped tablespoons Labneh (*see* page 47)

25g pine nuts, toasted

25g dried barberries

Heat the oil in a frying pan, add the onion and gently fry for around 5 minutes until starting to soften. Add the courgettes and the amba spice and cook for 10–15 minutes until the courgettes are cooked through and starting to brown.

Remove the pan from the heat and season with the lemon juice and the salt if needed.

Spread the labneh on to a serving dish, top with the courgettes and scatter with the toasted pine nuts and barberries to garnish.

I had to include two stuffed aubergine recipes in this book because I couldn't decide between this one and the Tomato-stuffed Aubergine with a Sourdough and Walnut Crumb on page 135. While they are both very different, they each celebrate how amazing this vegetable is as a vehicle for some really powerful flavour toppings.

Baba Ganoush-stuffed Aubergine with Tomato and Fennel Confit

Serves 4 as a main or 8 as a side

4 aubergines
100ml olive oil
16 small cherry tomatoes
2 small fennel bulbs, woody stalks and cores removed and fronds reserved to garnish, very thinly sliced (preferably with a mandolin if you have one)
1 green chilli, halved lengthways
1 tablespoon tahini
juice of ½ lemon
2 garlic cloves, very finely chopped
pinch of sea salt
50g feta cheese
freshly ground black pepper
1 tablespoon mint leaves, finely chopped

Preheat the oven to 180°C/160°C fan/Gas Mark 4.

If you have a gas hob, using a pair of tongs, hold each aubergine one at a time over a high flame to lightly char the skins, turning to ensure that all sides are charred; this will take no more than 5 minutes. Place on a baking tray. If you don't have a gas hob, preheat the grill to high. Place the aubergines on a baking tray lined with foil and cook for around 10–15 minutes, turning halfway through, until the skins have started to blister.

Bake the charred aubergines for 30 minutes until cooked through.

Meanwhile, add the oil to a frying pan with the tomatoes, fennel and green chilli and cook over a low heat for about 10 minutes until the tomatoes start to pop their skins and soften.

Remove the aubergines from the oven, and when they are cool enough to handle, halve them lengthways and carefully scoop out the flesh, making sure that you leave around a 2mm layer of flesh in the skins. Add the flesh to a bowl and mix with the tahini, lemon juice, garlic and salt.

Return the flesh mixture to the skins, using a slotted spoon to avoid adding excess oil, then spoon over the tomato and fennel confit.

Crumble the feta cheese over the top, add a twist of black pepper and garnish with the chopped mint and reserved fennel fronds. Serve at room temperature.

Schupfnudeln are potato noodles eaten in the same quantity by the Germans as gnocchi are by the Italians. Also known as *fingernudeln* due to their finger-like shape, the hand-rolled potato dough for these noodles is often made by my kids. They love rolling the dough with their small hands into little worm shapes and making a complete floury mess in the kitchen, but it's the creamy mushroom sauce with the buttery little noodles that they enjoy the most (even though they always claim to hate mushrooms).

Schupfnudeln with Creamy Mushroom Sauce

Serves 4

For the schupfnudeln

1kg floury potatoes, such as Maris Piper or King Edward, scrubbed

1 egg yolk

table salt

½ teaspoon ground white pepper

¼ teaspoon freshly grated nutmeg

300g plain flour, plus extra for dusting

60g potato flour

1 tablespoon rapeseed oil

25g butter

For the creamy mushroom sauce

1 tablespoon rapeseed oil

25g butter

2 shallots, finely diced

2 garlic cloves, very finely chopped

250g chestnut mushrooms, sliced

1 tablespoon thyme leaves, very finely chopped, plus 1 teaspoon for garnish

100ml Madeira wine

250ml vegetable stock (made using 1 teaspoon bouillon powder)

300ml double cream

½ teaspoon sea salt

a few twists of black pepper

Start by making the schupfnudeln. Cook the unpeeled potatoes in a large saucepan of boiling water for 20–25 minutes until very tender. Drain and leave to cool in a colander.

Peel and then mash the potatoes really well so that there are no lumps; a potato ricer would be best for this job.

Add the mash to a bowl and mix in the egg yolk, 1 teaspoon of table salt, white pepper and nutmeg. Then gently work in the flours, taking care not to overmix.

Turn the dough out on to a lightly floured work surface and roll into a long sausage shape about 2cm thick. Cut into 1cm-thick pieces and then roll each piece into a little pencil-shaped noodle.

Bring a large saucepan of salted water to the boil and add the noodles. As soon as they float to the surface, after around a minute, remove with a slotted spoon to a bowl of iced water.

For the sauce, heat the oil and butter in a large frying pan, add the shallots, garlic and mushrooms and fry over a medium heat for around 10 minutes, stirring frequently, until the mushrooms have softened. Add the thyme and cook for a further 2 minutes. Turn the heat up, add the Madeira and leave the mixture to bubble away for 5 minutes until the liquid has evaporated and the mushrooms have started to turn golden at the edges. Add the stock and cream and bring to the boil, then continue cooking over a medium heat for 8 minutes to reduce and thicken the sauce. Season with the salt and black pepper, cover and keep warm.

To fry the schupfnudeln, heat the oil in a large frying pan and add a small piece of the butter. Fry the noodles, in batches, over a medium-high heat for 2–3 minutes, shaking them around the pan, until they turn golden brown. Remove each fried batch of noodles with a slotted spoon and add a dot more butter to the pan before adding the next lot of noodles.

Divide the noodles between 4 shallow bowls, spoon over the mushroom sauce and garnish with the remaining teaspoon of thyme.

Dressings, pickles & sauces

I met a very talented pickle man called Nick Vadasz of Vadasz Deli at my local farmers' market. His Jewish grandmother, who left her native Hungary in the late 1950s, provided the inspiration for his pickling enterprise, and working out of his premises in Hackney, East London, he continues the family tradition by producing an amazing range of pickles, from kimchi to cucumbers. Having tried a few, I asked him very politely for his pickled red cabbage recipe, one of my favourites. To my amazement he kindly agreed, so I am delighted to share it with you. This will make a large quantity, but it keeps for up to 12 weeks in the fridge, and there's no harm in having a regular supply on hand.

Pickled Red Cabbage

Makes 4 x 1-litre jars

1 large red cabbage

For the brine
1.25 litres spirit vinegar
500g granulated sugar
125g sea salt
500ml water
3 teaspoons juniper berries, roughly crushed
2 teaspoons black peppercorns, roughly crushed
4 teaspoons caraway seeds
4 teaspoons dill seeds

Wash the jars thoroughly and then sterilize by running through the dishwater or placing them in a large pan of simmering water for about 5–10 minutes. Remove with tongs and leave to drain and dry.

For the brine, put the vinegar, sugar, salt and measured water into a large stainless steel saucepan and heat gently, stirring occasionally, until the sugar and salt have dissolved. Add all the spices to the hot brine.

Cut the cabbage in half and remove the core, then slice very thinly using a mandolin or food processor, or by hand.

Divide the cabbage between 4 × 1-litre preserving jars, filling each one half full. Pour over the hot brine and seal. Leave at room temperature for 24 hours before transferring to the fridge, then store for 1–2 weeks before eating.

Tahini is traditionally regarded as a condiment in the Middle East, much like tomato ketchup in the West, but it can also be used to bring a lovely Middle Eastern flavour to any dish. My fridge is never without a squeezy bottle full of this dressing, ready to drizzle over salads and meats or just to use as a dipping sauce for pretty much anything. The dense sesame paste is lightened here with some yogurt and fresh lemon juice.

Tahini Dressing

Makes 4 servings

100g tahini
100g natural yogurt
juice of ½ lemon
½ teaspoon sea salt

Mix the tahini and yogurt together in a bowl, then add the lemon juice and salt and whisk in.

Thin with water to achieve your desired consistency if using as a salad dressing or dipping sauce.

The dressing will keep in an airtight container in the fridge for up to 5 days.

Chrain holds a very poignant memory for me. One Seder night, the ritual feast that marks the start of Passover, my older sister and some very close family friends decided to play a trick on me. They told me (sorry, dared me) to take a large spoon of chrain and eat it on its own. Never one to pass up a dare, I did it, and when my face went as many shades of deep red as the chrain, they rolled about laughing, with the parents joining in too. I have still to this day never lived it down. Some 30 years later when I find myself making this very hot and tear-jerking condiment, I can't help but smile. This fiery red horseradish and beetroot combo is a particularly good accompaniment to Fried Fish Balls (*see* page 59) or cold meats.

Chrain

Serves 8

50g fresh horseradish root, peeled and chopped into chunks
1 red beetroot, around 120g, peeled and chopped into large pieces
2 teaspoons white wine vinegar
1 tablespoon fresh lemon juice
1 tablespoon caster sugar
1 teaspoon sea salt
freshly ground black pepper

Add the horseradish to a power blender and blend on the highest speed until it is almost like a paste.

Add the beetroot and blend again on high speed until completely chopped.

Add the remaining ingredients and give the mixture a final blitz, then taste (with a lot of caution!) to check for seasoning.

Transfer to a sterilized jar (*see* page 144) or airtight container, seal and store in the fridge until ready to serve. The chrain will keep for up to 4 weeks.

One of my greatest food experiences was travelling to Stockholm to cook in two of the country's most dynamic and cutting-edge restaurants. Sweden's cuisine sings to my heart with its pickles, curing, smoking, marinating – all the culinary techniques I love and want to learn more about. Given the very short summer season in Sweden, pickling is essential as a way of preserving the vegetables that have limited time to grow. The first thing I learned was how to make a classic pickling liquid and I've now adopted this recipe for all manner of vegetables, including fennel, radish and red onions. Attika vinegar is available through specialist online suppliers, but you could use a different spirit vinegar (not malt vinegar) as a substitute.

Sweet Pickled Beetroot

Makes 3 x 500ml jars

1kg beetroot
210ml Attika vinegar or spirit vinegar
300g caster sugar
650ml water

Wash and sterilize the jars (see page 144).

Remove the stalks from the beetroot and scrub well. Add to a saucepan and cover with cold water. Bring to the boil, then turn the heat down and simmer gently for around 25 minutes or until the point of a sharp knife goes in easily, depending on the size of the beetroot.

Drain and leave to cool, then carefully remove the skins with the back of a table knife. Chop into small cubes.

Put the vinegar, sugar and measured water into a large stainless steel saucepan and heat gently, stirring occasionally, until the sugar has dissolved. Leave to cool completely.

Divide the cubes of beetroot between 3 × 500ml preserving jars, top with the pickling liquid and seal. The beetroot is ready to eat straight away, or can be kept for up to 3 months in the fridge.

When I was growing up, our fridge was always full of pickled cucumbers, as they were part of our everyday condiments on the table for lunch and dinner. They were always Mrs Elswood ready-made pickles from the kosher section; my mum never thought about making her own. Given the vast quantity of cucumbers that my own family consumes, sheer economics led me on a quest to devise my own quick-and-easy concoction. The small Lebanese or Turkish cucumbers work so much better than English cucumbers because they are less watery and hold their crunch better. They can be found in any ethnic supermarket.

Dill Pickled Cucumbers

Makes 2 x 1-litre jars

175ml distilled white vinegar

3 tablespoons sea salt

3 tablespoons caster sugar

300ml cold water

8 small Lebanese or Turkish cucumbers, halved lengthways

4 large garlic cloves, peeled and halved

1½ tablespoons coriander seeds

1½ teaspoons mustard seeds

10 sprigs of dill

Wash and sterilize the jars (see page 144).

Put the vinegar, salt and sugar in a medium stainless steel saucepan and gently heat, stirring, until the sugar and salt have dissolved. Transfer the liquid to a bowl and whisk in the measured cold water. Leave the brine to cool, then refrigerate until needed.

Divide the cucumbers between 2 × 1-litre preserving jars, tall enough to hold the cucumber spears vertically, and then add the garlic, coriander and mustard seeds and the dill sprigs. Pour the brine equally over the cucumbers, topping up with cold water if necessary to cover the cucumbers.

Seal the jars and leave in the fridge for 24 hours before eating. They will keep for up to a month.

Sides & salads

This is the dish that I get asked to make all the time, so it seemed only fitting that I included this in my first ever signature offering on *MasterChef*. Thankfully, it was a triumph. Better known as an Egyptian peasant dish, the warm, comforting notes of the Lebanese spices and the hearty nature of the lentils make a little of this stretch a long way. It will stand as a meal in its own right accompanied by a simple cumin-spiced yogurt and a bowl of Israeli 'Chik Chak' Salad (*see* page 172), or for a special occasion I normally serve it with Lamb Ghormeh Sabzi (*see* page 92) and Tzimmes (*see* page 177). The caramelized onions are the highlight of this dish and I use flour to turn them a bit crispy, but feel free to omit it if you have a wheat intolerance; they will still be just as tasty.

Sephardi Rice with Vermicelli and Lentils

Serves 6–8

200g dried green lentils

2 tablespoons plain flour (optional)

sea salt

3 large onions, sliced into thin half-moons

4 tablespoons olive oil

50g unsalted butter

60g dried short vermicelli egg noodles

300g basmati rice

2 teaspoons Lebanese 7-spice Mix (*see* page 14)

600ml hot chicken or vegetable stock

vegetable oil, for deep-frying

2 shallots, sliced into thin rings, to garnish

freshly ground black pepper

Rinse the lentils really well, then place in a saucepan, cover with plenty of cold water and bring to the boil. Cover with a lid, turn the heat down and simmer for 20–25 minutes, checking after 15 minutes; the lentils should be cooked but not mushy. Drain and refresh under cold running water to stop any further cooking, then set aside.

Meanwhile, if using the flour, season with 1 teaspoon salt and spread out on a plate, then toss the onion slices in the seasoned flour to coat. Heat the olive oil in a large frying pan and gently fry the onions, in batches, for about 25 minutes until a rich dark brown colour. Remove with a slotted spoon and drain on a plate lined with kitchen paper.

Heat the butter in a large, heavy-based saucepan with a lid, and when it is sizzling, add the vermicelli, stirring constantly until it is just starting to brown. Add the rice and Lebanese 7-spice mix and stir everything together until the rice is nicely coated in the butter, then add the hot stock and bring to the boil. Cover with the lid and cook on the lowest heat possible for exactly 12 minutes. Turn the heat off, remove the lid and cover the pan with a clean tea towel, then replace the lid and leave to sit for 10 minutes, to help fluff up the grains.

For the garnish, pour the vegetable oil into a small, deep saucepan and add the shallots while it is still cold. Heat the oil; once it reaches a temperature of around 170°C, the shallots will crisp quite quickly, so stay near the pan. When they are golden brown, remove with a slotted spoon and drain on a plate lined with kitchen paper.

Add the lentils to the rice, then the caramelized onions and stir through with 2 forks to avoid the rice clumping together. Season with extra salt, if needed, and some black pepper. Tip the rice mixture into a large bowl and garnish with the crispy shallots.

My mother-in-law is one of nine siblings: seven brothers and two sisters. While two of her brothers came to live in the UK, the remaining three brothers and her sister stayed in Israel, and it's those siblings and their children who we make a concerted effort to go and see every other year with the kids. The thing I look forward to the most is the food. Whether it's a giant barbecue, a traditional High Holiday feast or just a Friday night dinner, the discussions around what we are going to eat, followed by who is going to make it and where we are eating, take a considerable amount of time and effort. The results are always sensational, and a few loosened belt notches later, I will inevitably be found following the chief cook around with my pen and paper, making note of the recipes. This was one of those that I scribbled down. First made for me by Aunty Rochele at my engagement party, this dish has been the talking point at just about every barbecue or buffet spread I've offered it up at ever since. It's very simple to make with just a few simple ingredients, and goes really well with the Tomato-stuffed Aubergine with a Sourdough and Walnut Crumb (*see* page 135) or the Chicken and Pistachio Meatballs with Coriander Tahini (*see* page 85).

Wild Rice Salad

Serves 6 as a main or 8–10 as a side

250g wild rice

250g long-grain rice

1 tablespoon sunflower oil

20 ripe cherry tomatoes, halved

100g raw cashew nuts

100g sun-dried tomatoes in oil, chopped into bite-sized pieces, plus some of the oil

100g pitted green olives, halved

2 large handfuls of basil leaves, finely chopped

sea salt and freshly ground black pepper

Rinse the wild rice and add to a large saucepan with about 900ml of salted boiling water. Boil for around 40–45 minutes, checking to ensure that the grains have popped but still retain some bite.

While the wild rice is cooking, rinse the long-grain rice and add to a separate large saucepan with about 1.25 litres boiling water and a pinch of salt. Pop the lid on and cook over a low heat for around 12–15 minutes or until cooked but still slightly al dente. Drain the rice and leave to cool.

Heat 1 teaspoon of the oil in a frying pan, add the cherry tomatoes and cook over a high heat for a couple of minutes or until they just start to break down at the edges. Remove from the pan and set aside. Add the cashew nuts to the pan and fry until they just start to colour slightly, then set aside.

To assemble the salad, mix the cooked wild and long-grain rice together in a large bowl, then add the sun-dried tomatoes and olives, using a few drops of the oil from the tomatoes to coat the salad slightly. Add the chopped basil and season to taste with sea salt and black pepper. Serve at room temperature.

A lovely and very talented friend of mine, Nikita Gulhane, runs the Spice Monkey Indian cookery school in North London and once offered this rice dish as part of an incredible lunch spread. I had just had my first baby and we were gathering for our antenatal class mums' (and sometimes dads') weekly get-together. I hadn't cooked for a while and was desperate to find tasty and easy meals I could prepare while juggling the demands of a small and needy child. This spicy mushroom rice was the most adventurous dish I could muster while caring for my newborn baby. Nikita told me what ingredients he used and I then went away and constructed a recipe from it. Minimal fuss; maximum taste. This is great served with the Turmeric-battered Cauliflower with Chilli and Saffron Yogurt (*see* page 168).

Spicy Mushroom and Cashew Nut Rice

Serves 4

1 tablespoon vegetable oil

1½ teaspoons cumin seeds

½ teaspoon ground turmeric

½ teaspoon chilli flakes

thumb-sized piece of fresh root ginger, peeled and finely chopped

1 small white onion, finely chopped

1 fat garlic clove, finely chopped

150g chestnut mushrooms, sliced

50g raw cashew nuts, halved

200g basmati rice

400ml boiling water

1 teaspoon sea salt

freshly ground black pepper

Heat the oil in a saucepan over a medium heat, throw in the cumin seeds, turmeric, chilli flakes and ginger and cook, stirring, for a couple of minutes. Then add the onion and cook with the spices until it is softened. Add the garlic, mushrooms and cashew nuts and cook for a few more minutes, then tip in the rice and stir, making sure that the grains are nicely coated in the oil and spices.

Pour in the measured boiling water and season with the salt and a few twists of black pepper. Bring to the boil, then pop a lid on, turn the heat down to its lowest setting and cook for 10 minutes.

Turn the heat off and leave the rice, with the lid on, to steam for a further 10 minutes before serving.

These are definitely what you would call special occasion potatoes. The recipe is a Lebanese take on my father-in-law's little crispy fried potatoes, and works really well as an accompaniment to a robust meat such as lamb or beef.

Chilli and Coriander Fried Potatoes

Serves 6

6 large white floury potatoes, such as Maris Piper or King Edward, peeled and cut into small cubes

100ml vegetable or sunflower oil

1 red onion, finely diced

2 garlic cloves, finely chopped

1 red chilli, deseeded and finely chopped (leave the seeds in if you want more heat)

1 teaspoon ground coriander

½ teaspoon ground cumin

2 large handfuls of fresh coriander, finely chopped

sea salt and freshly ground black pepper

Blanch the potatoes in a large saucepan of salted boiling water for 5 minutes. Drain and leave to dry.

If your frying pan isn't large enough to hold the potatoes in a single layer, do this next step in batches; just divide up the oil. Heat the oil over a medium-high heat, and when it has almost reached smoking point, carefully add the potatoes (wear an apron and stand well back) and fry for around 10 minutes, turning every so often, so that they colour evenly.

Add the onion, garlic, chilli and spices, season with sea salt and black pepper and fry for a further 5 minutes until the potatoes are nicely crisp and golden and cooked through. Finish by adding the fresh coriander (reserving a little for garnish) and stir through. Serve the potatoes hot, garnished with the reserved coriander.

Tip

If I'm cooking for spice-averse kids as well, I divide the amount of potatoes I've blanched in half and roast their half in some sunflower oil on a baking tray in an oven preheated to 200°C/180°C fan/Gas Mark 6 for around 30 minutes, turning frequently.

I used to enjoy latkes every Chanukah, when they are traditionally served to symbolize the miracle of oil (yes, oily foods are the done thing during this festival), along with cheese blintzes and doughnuts. The key to achieving the perfect latke is to make sure the oil is not so hot that the potato burns before it is properly cooked, but hot enough that it crisps up nicely. The topping choices are vast and include Salt Beef (*see* page 106) and pickles or Lox (*see* page 39) and soured cream. Alternatively, simply enjoy them on their own, snatched quickly out of the pan and eaten between sheets of kitchen paper the way I did.

Fennel and Potato Latkes with Lemon and Chive Aioli

Makes 20 latkes

1 fennel bulb
4 white potatoes, around 1kg in total
1 onion
2 teaspoons fennel seeds, crushed with a pestle and mortar
3 large eggs, beaten
80g plain flour or medium matzo meal
2 teaspoons sea salt
freshly ground black pepper
100ml sunflower oil, for frying

For the lemon and chive aioli
5 tablespoons mayonnaise
juice of ½ lemon
1 garlic clove, crushed
1 tablespoon finely chopped chives

Preheat the oven to 110°C/90°C fan/Gas Mark ¼.

Cut the woody stalk off the fennel bulb, then cut the bulb in half lengthways. Remove the core and slice very thinly, preferably with a mandolin if you have one. Add the fennel slices to a bowl of cold water and leave to soften for 10 minutes.

Peel the potatoes and grate coarsely or, even better, use the grating attachment on your food processor if you have one. Peel and grate the onion, then add with the potato to a clean tea towel and squeeze as much of the liquid out as possible.

Add the potato and onion to a large bowl. Drain the fennel and add to the bowl with the crushed fennel seeds, eggs, flour or matzo meal, salt and some black pepper. Mix really well with your hands.

Heat 80ml of the oil in a large frying pan over a medium heat. When the oil is hot but not smoking, add about 3 tablespoonfuls of the mixture per latke to the pan and flatten with a spatula. Fry the latkes, turning once, for around 4–5 minutes on each side until a deep golden brown. Remove with a slotted spoon to a baking tray lined with kitchen paper and keep warm in the oven while you fry the rest. Repeat with the remaining latke mixture, adding a bit more of the remaining oil each time.

Meanwhile, mix all the ingredients for the aioli together well in a bowl.

Serve the latkes warm on a large plate with a bowl of the aioli on the side.

Tip

You can store any leftover latkes in a single layer on a baking tray in the fridge and then reheat in an oven preheated to 200°C/180°C fan/ Gas Mark 6 for 20–30 minutes.

This is a lovely twist on a classic potato salad and it's my barbecue or picnic table staple. The crunch and sharpness from the spicy cucumber pairs really nicely with the soft creamy potatoes and egg. You will find the Beit Hashita Cucumbers in most major supermarkets in the kosher section or at Middle Eastern grocers, but if you can't get these, any type of pickled cucumber or cornichon would work well.

New Potato and Egg Salad with Spicy Cucumbers

Serves 8

1kg baby new potatoes, scrubbed

4 hard-boiled eggs

6 Beit Hashita Cucumbers in Brine or other pickled cucumbers (or use 12 cornichons)

1 teaspoon sea salt

freshly ground black pepper

6 spring onions, thinly sliced

4–6 tablespoons good-quality mayonnaise

Cook the potatoes in a large saucepan of boiling water for around 12–15 minutes until cooked through. Drain and leave to cool, then scrape off the skins. Halve any larger potatoes so that you end up with them all roughly the same size.

Shell and chop the eggs and cucumbers into rough dice, then add to a large bowl with the salt and some black pepper, the spring onions (reserving a few slices for garnish) and mayonnaise. Add the potatoes and mix well.

Serve the salad garnished with the reserved spring onions and a couple of extra twists of black pepper.

Tips

* I prefer to buy small new potatoes and cook them in their skins for extra flavour, then scrape off the skins once cooled, but you can of course leave the skins on to reduce the work involved a little; the result is equally tasty.

* For an extra flavour punch, add a crushed large garlic clove to the mayo.

Cauliflower is having what you would call 'a moment', with many menus now offering it as a dish in its own right, elevating it from humble side vegetable to queen of the plate. Its versatility makes it a great vegetable to experiment with, and that's exactly what I was doing when this recipe came about. Fried, roasted, baked, mashed or blitzed into couscous, it's like a flavour sponge, gracefully accepting whatever dressing you throw on it. As a cook, I often think of flavour first, texture second and visual impact third. This dish is the perfect result of the three: the tenderness of the cauliflower with the earthy and slightly tangy flavour of the za'atar and barberries, against the soft couscous and crunchy almonds. Enjoy this as a hearty lunch or supper. If you struggle to find barberries, you can replace them with dried cranberries, raisins or dried sour cherries.

Pan-fried Cauliflower with Caramelized Red Onions, Toasted Israeli Couscous and Almonds

Serves 6

80ml olive oil

1 large red onion, thinly sliced into half-moons

2 tablespoons soft dark brown sugar

2 tablespoons balsamic vinegar

1 large or 2 small cauliflowers, cut into large florets, any small leaves retained

150g toasted Israeli couscous (or substitute fregola if you can't find it)

500ml hot chicken or vegetable stock

40g butter, cut into pieces

2–3 tablespoons Za'atar (see page 15)

1 tablespoon Lebanese 7-spice Mix (see page 14)

100g raw unblanched almonds

50g pine nuts, lightly toasted

2 large handfuls of dried barberries

sea salt and freshly ground black pepper

To garnish

generous sprinkling of pomegranate seeds

a few oregano leaves

Heat 2 tablespoons of the oil in a frying pan, add the onion and gently fry for 10–15 minutes with a pinch of salt until caramelized, stirring occasionally. Add the sugar and vinegar and cook for 5–10 minutes more until slightly sticky.

Meanwhile, blanch the cauliflower and its leaves in a large saucepan of salted boiling water for 3–4 minutes. Drain and leave to steam dry in a colander.

Heat a tablespoon of the remaining oil in a saucepan over a medium heat, add the couscous and stir to coat. Fry for around 2–3 minutes, then cover with the hot stock and add a pinch of salt. Bring to the boil, then cover and simmer for around 8–10 minutes. Drain off any liquid and set aside.

Heat the remaining oil in a frying pan over a medium heat, add the cauliflower and fry, turning occasionally, for 10 minutes or until golden and cooked through. Drain off any oil from the pan and set the cauliflower aside.

Place the pan back on the heat and add the butter, za'atar and Lebanese spice mix. Stir until the butter has melted, then add the cauliflower back in and baste until it is well coated. Throw in the almonds, pine nuts and barberries and stir everything in the pan until it has all heated through.

Transfer the cauliflower mixture to a large bowl and mix through the couscous and the cooked red onion. Season with some sea salt and black pepper, and garnish with the pomegranate seeds and oregano leaves. The dish can be served hot or at room temperature.

Tip

The couscous and onion can be made up to 24 hours ahead and the cauliflower blanched in advance, so don't worry about having to tackle all the elements at the same time.

Crispy and lightly spiced, this dish makes a lovely sharing plate for a starter, or a pre-dinner nibble. You want the cauliflower florets to be bite-sized, but not too small that they can't take on the batter.

Turmeric-battered Cauliflower with Chilli and Saffron Yogurt

Serves 4

1 cauliflower, cut into florets
vegetable or rapeseed oil,
for deep-frying

For the yogurt
small pinch of saffron threads
3 tablespoons hot water
200g Greek yogurt
juice of ½ lemon
¼ teaspoon Aleppo pepper
1 garlic clove, crushed
pinch of sea salt

For the batter
1 tablespoon nigella seeds
1 tablespoon ground turmeric
165g self-raising flour
210ml chilled sparkling water
1 teaspoon table salt

For the garnish
handful of picked coriander leaves,
roughly chopped
1 tablespoon pomegranate molasses

Blanch the cauliflower in a large saucepan of salted boiling water for 2 minutes, then drain in a colander and refresh under cold running water to stop any further cooking.

For the yogurt, infuse the saffron in the measured hot water for 20 minutes, then strain out the saffron and discard. Mix the saffron water into the yogurt and add the remaining yogurt ingredients. Cover and refrigerate until ready to serve.

Heat the oil for deep-frying in a deep-fat fryer or medium saucepan (ensure that the oil is a minimum of 5cm deep, but don't fill the pan more than halfway) and place over a medium heat to heat up to around 170°C.

Meanwhile, whisk all the ingredients for the batter together in a bowl until you have a thick consistency.

Test the temperature of the oil by dropping in a little of the batter – if it sizzles, the oil is ready. Dip the cauliflower florets in the batter to coat, shaking off the excess, and fry, in small batches, for 4 minutes. Remove with a slotted spoon to a plate lined with kitchen paper.

Transfer to a serving plate and garnish with the coriander and pomegranate molasses, with the yogurt on the side for dipping.

The season for these delicious little morsels is annoyingly short, so I make the most of them during their brief winter appearance. This recipe was born out of one of many experimental sessions trying to find a suitable partner for them. In this case, crisp French beans and some gently cooked red onions did the job really well; add to that the creamy tarragon dressing and it's mouth-wateringly good. I've served this as a starter for my supper clubs to high acclaim, and it's sure to convert anyone put off by Jerusalem artichokes' rather intimidating appearance into cooking with them.

Roasted Jerusalem Artichokes and French Bean Salad

Serves 6

500g Jerusalem artichokes
6 tablespoons olive oil
2 tablespoons lemon thyme leaves (or 2 teaspoons dried thyme if you can't get hold of it)
1 large red onion, thinly sliced into half-moons
200g French beans
150g bag of pea shoots or watercress
sea salt

For the dressing
3 black garlic cloves, peeled
6 tablespoons double cream
2 tablespoons fresh lemon juice
2 tablespoons finely chopped tarragon
freshly ground black pepper

Preheat the oven to 180°C/160°C fan/Gas Mark 4.

Scrub the artichokes really well and remove any knobbly bits. Cut into wedges and place on a baking tray with 3 tablespoons of the olive oil, the thyme and a teaspoon of salt, tossing everything together really well to ensure that everything is coated in the oil. Roast for 25–30 minutes, then increase the heat to 200°C/180°C fan/Gas Mark 6 and roast for a further 10 minutes until cooked through and golden, turning 2 or 3 times during the process. Remove from the oven and leave to cool slightly.

Warm the remaining 3 tablespoons of olive oil in a frying pan, add the onion with a pinch of salt and cook over a really low heat for around 10 minutes until soft and translucent. Set aside.

Cook the French beans in a saucepan of salted boiling water for around 3 minutes until just al dente, then drain and refresh under cold running water to stop any further cooking.

To make the dressing, pound the black garlic into a paste using a pestle and mortar or with the back of a spoon. Mix the garlic into the cream and whisk with the remaining dressing ingredients, reserving a little of the tarragon for garnish, then season with a good few twists of black pepper and set aside.

To assemble the salad, place the pea shoots or watercress on a plate, arrange the artichokes, onion and French beans nicely on top and drizzle the dressing all over. Garnish with the reserved tarragon and serve.

Tip

This salad is best served at room temperature, so make everything ahead but don't dress it until just before you serve. If you can't find black garlic, the dressing will taste almost as good without it.

This salad is served for breakfast, lunch and dinner in Israel, in every home, restaurant, market and café. I first learned the art of chopping (yes, that's the only skill required here) this salad while working on a kibbutz aged 19 in the far north of Israel. Working in the kitchen was a job reserved for the residents (kibbutzniks) only, not the working guests, but I pretty much begged to help out one day and this was the task I was given – chopping enough vegetables for a salad to feed 200 people. I loved every minute, setting myself the challenge of chopping each vegetable as uniformly and precisely as possible. That is the art here, making sure all the vegetables are the same size and nice and small. See this as a therapeutic job and not a chore, and you will enjoy it so much more.

Israeli 'Chik Chak' Salad

Serves 4 as a side

1 whole cucumber

6 ripe plum tomatoes or 200g baby plum tomatoes

100g radishes

½ yellow pepper

100g green olives stuffed with jalapeño (I like Fragata) or pimento

½ red onion

For the dressing

juice of 1 lemon (squeeze over half to begin with, then add the remainder if needed)

3 tablespoons good-quality extra virgin olive oil, plus extra if needed

½ teaspoon sea salt

freshly ground black pepper (be generous)

1 teaspoon ground sumac

Split the cucumber in half lengthways and deseed. Cut the tomatoes in half and scoop out the seeds (if you are using baby plum tomatoes, you don't need to remove the seeds). Top and tail the radishes and core and deseed the pepper.

Dice all the vegetables the same size and as small as you possibly can.

Add to a bowl with all the dressing ingredients, then add more oil and lemon juice if needed; you want it to be nice and sharp.

Serve with just about anything.

Halloumi is one of my favourite cheeses and za'atar is one of my favourite spices, so it felt only right to put the two together. I always dust the halloumi slices with cornflour so that they immediately crust when they hit the hot pan. This is a simple yet really delicious salad that makes an impressive vegetarian starter, or a lovely addition to a buffet spread.

Za'atar-crusted Halloumi Salad with a Lime and Mint Dressing

Serves 4

1 large fennel bulb, woody stalk removed and very thinly sliced (preferably with a mandolin if you have one)
1 heaped tablespoon cornflour
2 tablespoons Za'atar (see page 15)
300g halloumi cheese
I tablespoon olive oil
seeds from ½ pomegranate, to garnish

For the dressing
6 tablespoons olive oil
1 teaspoon white balsamic vinegar
juice of 1 lime
10 mint leaves, finely chopped
2 teaspoons Za'atar (see page 15)
pinch of sea salt
freshly ground black pepper

Place the sliced fennel in a bowl, cover with cold water and leave to soften for 10 minutes, then drain.

Mix the cornflour and za'atar together on a plate, then spread out. Slice the halloumi and roll in the seasoned flour to coat.

Heat the olive oil in a frying pan over a high heat, and when it is really hot, add the halloumi and fry, undisturbed, for 1–2 minutes, then turn and cook on the other side for a further minute. Remove to a plate.

Add all the ingredients for the dressing, reserving some of the mint for garnish, to a bowl or, even better, a screw-top jar and give them a good whisk or screw on the lid and shake to combine.

Add the fennel slices to a shallow bowl, top with the halloumi and drizzle over the dressing. Garnish with the reserved mint and the pomegranate seeds and serve immediately.

Tzimmes is a classic High Holiday dish, most traditionally eaten on Passover and Rosh Hashanah, and there are dozens of variations above and beyond the carrot and cinnamon version that I've given here. My mum used to make this dish in an attempt to get my sisters and me to eat carrots. Dressing them up in lots of butter and cinnamon certainly helps, but throw in some raisins and then you're talking. For this recipe, I felt it was sweet enough without the addition of any dried fruit, but feel free to add them if you're trying to lure in fussy kids. This is great served with Friday Night Chicken with Onions and Roast Potatoes (*see* page 79).

Tzimmes

Serves 4

2 tablespoons rapeseed oil

1 white onion, thinly sliced

1 teaspoon freshly grated nutmeg

1 teaspoon ground cinnamon

1 teaspoon fennel seeds

½ teaspoon sea salt

4 large carrots, peeled and cut lengthways, then chopped into 1cm-thick half discs

30g butter

300ml water

grated zest and juice of 1 orange

2 tablespoons date syrup

1 red chilli, deseeded and finely chopped

1 tablespoon finely chopped flat leaf parsley

juice of ½ lemon

Heat the oil in a wide, heavy-based saucepan, add the onion, nutmeg, cinnamon, fennel seeds and salt and sauté over a medium heat for about 10 minutes until the onion is soft and translucent. Stir in the carrots and butter and cook for 2 minutes.

Add the measured water, orange zest and juice and date syrup, cover with a lid and cook for 30 minutes or until the carrots are soft.

Take the lid off and cook for a further 5 minutes to reduce the liquid into a syrupy mass.

Add the chilli, parsley and lemon juice to finish before serving.

Sweet, salty and spicy all on one plate; this dish is a great hit of powerful flavours that all mesh really well together. *Zhoug* is a fiery Middle Eastern relish that works as a condiment for all manner of dishes, so store any leftover sauce in an airtight container in the fridge for up to two weeks.

Caramelized Butternut Squash with Whipped Feta and Zhoug

Serves 4

1 large butternut squash, peeled, deseeded and cut into 2cm chunks

30g butter, melted

1 tablespoon soft dark brown sugar

1 teaspoon ground cinnamon

½ teaspoon sea salt

30g unsalted pistachio nuts

100g Whipped Feta (*see* page 46)

For the zhoug

1 bunch of coriander, including stalks

½ bunch of flat leaf parsley, stalks removed

1 green chilli

1 tablespoon chilli flakes

½ teaspoon ground cumin

½ teaspoon ground coriander

½ teaspoon sea salt

100ml rapeseed oil

juice of ½ lemon

Preheat the oven to 200°C/180°C fan/Gas Mark 6.

Place the butternut squash in a bowl and toss with the melted butter, sugar, cinnamon and salt. Spread out on a baking tray and roast for 30 minutes or until cooked through and the sugar is starting to caramelize.

While the squash is roasting, add the pistachios to a separate baking tray and roast for 8 minutes or until they begin to brown and smell nutty. Remove from the oven and leave to cool, then chop roughly with a knife.

For the zhoug, place all the ingredients except the lemon juice in a food processor and pulse until it forms a loose green sauce. Stir in the lemon juice.

Once cooked, transfer the butternut squash to a serving dish and dot over tablespoonfuls of the whipped feta before drizzling over the spicy zhoug and scattering with the chopped nuts.

This is a very quick and easy salad to prepare and is a perfect accompaniment to cold meats, salmon or as part of a meze platter. Although this salad can be served straight away, it's much better left in the fridge for a few hours to allow the onion to soften a little and for the flavours to develop. It goes perfectly with Lox (*see* page 39), or serve as part of a spread with Chopped Liver (*see* page 63) or Egg and Onion (*see* page 62).

Hungarian Cucumber Salad

Serves 4

2 large green cucumbers
1 large white onion, very thinly sliced
1 teaspoon table salt
3 tablespoons caster sugar
5 tablespoons white wine or cider vinegar
3 tablespoons water
large handful of dill, finely chopped

Trim and thinly slice the cucumbers, then add to a large bowl along with the onion and salt. Toss together and leave to sit for 10 minutes.

Add the sugar, vinegar, measured water and dill to the bowl, then mix all the ingredients together, ensuring that everything is well combined.

Cover and chill in the fridge for a few hours or longer (it only gets better) until you are ready to serve.

I would love to think of a way to make this sound more appetizing than 'cabbage salad' – it doesn't exactly jump off the page and scream, 'Make me!' But it really is one of the tastiest cabbage salads you will ever eat. With no more than five ingredients, I guarantee you will have your guests clamouring for the recipe. I've kept this guarded for 14 years, ever since I prised it off my husband's Israeli aunt after she made the dish for our engagement party. I now feel the need to share; some things are too good to keep to yourself.

Aunty Rochele's Cabbage Salad

Serves 8 as part of a meze spread

1 large white cabbage
4 tablespoons balsamic vinegar
4 tablespoons soft dark brown sugar
4 tablespoons soy sauce
4 tablespoons sunflower oil
3 tablespoons sesame seeds
50g pine nuts

Shred the cabbage finely – the grating attachment on your food processor will do the job nicely if you have one. Rinse and set aside to drain, as you want it dry before you add the dressing.

Heat the vinegar, sugar and soy sauce slowly in a saucepan until the sugar has dissolved, then leave to cool before adding the sunflower oil.

Transfer the cabbage to a large bowl, add the dressing and give it a good mix – this can sit for a while to allow the flavours to meld before you serve.

Heat a dry frying pan, add the sesame seeds and pine nuts and toast over a medium heat until lightly golden and fragrant, shaking the pan constantly. Set aside and add to the salad just before serving.

This is a simple, tasty and great-looking colourful dish to adorn any buffet table. The earthiness of the beetroot stands up really well against the cabbage, and paired with the mustardy tang of the dressing, it's a lovely accompaniment to Salt Beef (*see* page 106) and Fennel and Potato Latkes (*see* page 162). In fact, I served this exact combo for one of my supper clubs and it was a real winner among the guests.

Red Cabbage, Black Olive and Beetroot Coleslaw

Serves 8

1 red cabbage
2 red beetroot, peeled
100g pitted black olives, sliced

For the dressing
200g crème fraîche or soured cream
1 tablespoon Dijon mustard
1 small red onion, very finely chopped
2 tablespoons balsamic vinegar
1 tablespoon date syrup
½ teaspoon sea salt
freshly ground black pepper

Cut the cabbage in half and remove the core, then shred finely – use the grating attachment on your food processor if you have one. Grate the beetroot on the large holes of a box grater and combine with the cabbage in a large bowl. Add the sliced olives and set aside.

Whisk all the ingredients for the dressing together in a bowl, cover and leave in the fridge for around 20 minutes to allow the flavours to mesh.

Add the dressing to the slaw just before serving and toss through.

This dish is inspired by a lovely Mediterranean restaurant close to where I live where they offer something very similar on the menu. Although the tapenade is a combination of bold flavours, it nevertheless allows this wonderful green vegetable to be the star of the plate. You can serve this side dish hot or cold, so it's an ideal prepare-ahead option.

Tenderstem Broccoli with Black Olive Tapenade

Serves 4

200g Tenderstem broccoli
2 small garlic cloves, peeled
100g pitted black olives
2 tablespoons capers
juice of ½ lemon, or to taste
small handful of flat leaf parsley, finely chopped
freshly ground black pepper
3 tablespoons good-quality extra virgin olive oil, plus extra for drizzling

Blanch the broccoli in a saucepan of boiling water for 90 seconds, then drain and set aside.

Finely chop the garlic, olives and capers together (a mezzaluna is a really great tool to use here if you have one). Add to a bowl with the lemon juice, parsley, a few twists of black pepper and 2 tablespoons of the olive oil. Taste and adjust the seasoning, and if necessary add more lemon juice.

Heat a frying pan over a medium-high heat, add the remaining tablespoon of oil and quickly flash-fry the broccoli until it is heated through; you want to ensure that it still retains a bite, so don't overcook it.

Place the broccoli on a plate and top with the tapenade and a good drizzle of extra virgin olive oil.

My husband and I united over our love of food, although it was actually our mutual dislike of certain combinations that made us realize how much we had in common. Fruit with savoury was the biggest offender, yet here I am promoting the one salad that made me reconsider my food demons. It's lovely and light, making a fantastic accompaniment to my Salmon and Sweet Potato Fishcakes (*see* page 119) and Spiced Cod Falafel (*see* page 43).

Fennel, Orange and Carrot Salad

Serves 4

1 fennel bulb, cut in half lengthways and very thinly sliced (preferably with a mandolin if you have one)

1 teaspoon coriander seeds

2 carrots, peeled and shaved into strips with a vegetable peeler

1 orange, peeled, segmented and cut into small chunks

handful of mint leaves, finely chopped

1 tablespoon extra virgin olive oil

juice of ½ lime

sea salt and freshly ground black pepper

Place the sliced fennel in a bowl, cover with cold water and leave to soften for 10 minutes, then drain.

Place a dry pan over a medium heat, add the coriander seeds and toast until they start to smell fragrant, shaking the pan constantly. Grind to a coarse powder with a pestle and mortar.

Transfer the drained fennel to a large bowl, add the carrots, orange, mint leaves and coriander and toss together. Dress the salad with the oil, lime juice and salt and black pepper to taste before serving.

Inspiration for this salad came from a very traditional Jewish dish called *kasha varnishkes*. Otherwise known as buckwheat, kasha is a gluten-free grain similar in appearance to freekeh and offers a protein-rich alternative to carb-heavy grains such as couscous or rice. Its nutty flavour lends itself really well to this powerful dressing. Serve as an accompaniment to Sticky Pomegranate Salmon (*see* page 117).

Buckwheat and Barberry Salad with Spiced Pomegranate Dressing

Serves 6 as a main or 8 as a side

200g buckwheat

150ml hot vegetable or chicken stock

50g unsalted pistachio nuts, roughly chopped

2 tablespoons dried barberries

1 teaspoon dried mint

1 tablespoon olive oil

2 large handfuls of coriander, finely chopped

For the pomegranate dressing

1 tablespoon date syrup

1 tablespoon pomegranate molasses

juice of 1 lemon

1 teaspoon ground cumin

1 teaspoon ground sumac

½ teaspoon grated fresh root ginger

½ teaspoon Harissa (*see* page 17)

sea salt and freshly ground black pepper

Place the buckwheat in a sieve and rinse really well in cold water. Add to a medium saucepan and cover with the hot stock. Bring to the boil, then cover with a lid and simmer gently for 10–12 minutes until the buckwheat is soft but still retains a little bite.

Drain and spread out on a tray or a plate to cool slightly (this avoids it ending up as one big sticky mass).

Whisk the ingredients for the dressing together in a bowl and set aside.

Transfer the buckwheat to a large bowl, then stir in the pistachios, barberries and mint, pour over the dressing and mix through with a fork. Finish with the olive oil and coriander, reserving a tablespoon of the latter for garnish. Serve at room temperature, scattered with the reserved coriander.

Sweets & baking

Some of the best recipes come out of being forced to experiment. Clean out of self-raising and plain flour, I only had wholemeal spelt flour in my store cupboard, which my wheat-free husband uses to make bread. I then decided to try and use up the catering-sized tub of natural yogurt in the fridge and whatever citrus fruit I had. The result was this delicious cake that is lovely and moist and, once topped with yogurt icing and pistachios, becomes wonderfully sticky. I was fortunate enough to inherit Grandma Celia's kugelhopf tin, which has to be at least 60 years old, and while I'm not quite the baker she was, the tin can make anything look impressive.

Yogurt, Pistachio and Orange Kugelhopf

Serves 8

250g caster sugar

3 large eggs

grated zest and juice of 2 large oranges

300g wholemeal or white spelt flour, plus extra for dusting

75g unsalted pistachio nuts, ground

2 teaspoons baking powder

1 teaspoon ground cinnamon

270g full-fat natural yogurt, plus 2 tablespoons for the icing

125ml vegetable oil, plus extra for greasing

For the topping

75g icing sugar

25g unsalted pistachio nuts, roughly chopped

Preheat the oven to 180°C/160°C fan/Gas Mark 4. Oil and flour a kugelhopf or bundt tin really well.

Whisk the sugar and eggs together in a stand mixer fitted with the whisk attachment or in a bowl with an electric whisk until light and fluffy; this will take around 10 minutes. Add the orange zest and juice and give the mixture one final mix before folding in the flour, ground pistachios, baking powder, cinnamon, the 270g yogurt and oil; don't overmix.

Pour the cake mixture into the prepared tin and bake for 40–45 minutes until a skewer inserted into the centre of the cake comes out clean. Leave to cool completely in the tin before turning out on to a plate.

While the cake is cooling, mix the remaining 2 tablespoons yogurt and icing sugar together in a bowl until you have a loose paste of pouring consistency.

Once you have unmoulded the cooled cake, generously drizzle the icing all over the top, allowing it to spill down the sides and form a puddle in the middle and around the outside. Sprinkle the chopped pistachios over the top and serve.

You wouldn't necessarily see cheesecake as a spiritual thing, that is unless you are Jewish. This ubiquitous dessert is the subject of many a Jewish argument as to its origins, about which there lots of different opinions and very little consensus. My food hero Claudia Roden once said that cheesecake was one of the first foods that Jews assimilated from their Central European neighbours. The famous New York-style baked cheesecake may be popular among many cheesecake fans, but the lesser-known Israeli version is something quite spectacular.

I make this cheesecake a lot, as it knows no boundaries in terms of the type of occasion it's appropriate for. I make catering-sized trays of it for parties and it never fails to receive a chorus of praise from the lucky recipients. Because it's a no-bake cheesecake, it means there is little that can go wrong. Just ensure that you use good-quality cream cheese and don't try using any other kind of biscuit – they are the key ingredient. This needs no accompaniment other than some fresh raspberries to cut through the sweetness. It's rich, velvety and incredibly moreish, so eat with caution.

Israeli White Chocolate Cheesecake

Makes around 12 slices, or 10 if you're greedy

200g petit beurre biscuits
120g unsalted butter, melted
150g white chocolate, broken into pieces
200g unsalted butter, softened
125g caster sugar
1 large egg
1 large egg yolk
250g good-quality cream cheese (I recommend Philadelphia)
200g full-fat crème fraîche

To prepare the biscuit base, add the biscuits to a food processor and blitz to crumbs, then mix with the melted butter.

Press two-thirds of the mixture into a 20 × 27cm baking dish, flattening it out so that it forms an even layer. Place in the freezer for 15 minutes until it is set.

Meanwhile, prepare the filling. Put the chocolate in a glass bowl and either set over a saucepan of simmering water, ensuring that the base of the bowl doesn't touch the water, or heat in the microwave in 30-second bursts, until melted. Remove the bowl from the pan and leave to cool slightly.

While the chocolate is melting and cooling, beat the softened butter, sugar, whole egg and egg yolk together in a stand mixer fitted with the paddle attachment until fluffy (or in a bowl with a wooden spoon and develop some muscle at the same time!); this will take around 10 minutes.

Beat the cream cheese and crème fraîche together in a bowl, then stir in the melted chocolate. Add to the butter and sugar mixture, then carefully fold all the ingredients together.

Spread the mixture evenly over the biscuit base and top with the remaining biscuit crumbs. Leave to set in the fridge for a minimum of 3 hours, but 24 hours is preferable.

An overabundance of apples every year from my tree encourages me to devise creative new ways of using them up. These muffins are an occasional weekend treat for the family, but more often I take them as a gift when joining friends for breakfast, brunch or lunch.

Apple and Cinnamon Muffins

Makes 12 muffins

260g plain flour
200g caster sugar
2 teaspoons baking powder
1 tablespoon ground cinnamon
½ teaspoon table salt
1 large eating apple, peeled, cored and very finely chopped
225ml buttermilk
60g butter, melted
2 eggs

For the crumble topping
75g soft dark brown sugar
30g plain flour
½ teaspoon ground cinnamon
1 tablespoon melted butter

Preheat the oven to 180°C/160°C fan/Gas Mark 4 and line a 12-cup muffin tin with paper muffin cases.

Whisk the flour, caster sugar, baking powder, cinnamon and salt together in a large bowl, then stir in the chopped apple.

Whisk the buttermilk, melted butter and eggs together, then stir through the flour mixture gently; don't overmix.

Fill each muffin case three-quarters full with the mixture. Mix all the crumble ingredients together in a small bowl with a fork, then sprinkle generously over the top of each muffin.

Bake for 18 minutes until the tops are golden brown and a skewer, when inserted, comes out clean. Leave to cool in the tin for a further 5 minutes.

Tip

Muffins always look extra impressive when baked in brown tulip-shaped paper cases.

Better known as cinnamon balls, these are the ultimate Passover baked treat. I would make them all the time when I was younger; now I delegate the task to my kids. When they make them they get a little over-excited and end up squishing them heavy-handedly rather than gently flattening them. It means I end up with all sorts of shapes and sizes, but they taste just as good. These are really easy to make and are a brilliant way to use up surplus egg whites.

Cinnamon Biscuits

Makes 20 biscuits

2 egg whites
200g ground almonds
120g caster sugar
1 tablespoon ground cinnamon, plus 1 teaspoon
3 tablespoons icing sugar

Preheat the oven to 180°C/160°C fan/Gas Mark 4 and line 2 baking trays with greaseproof paper.

Whisk the egg whites in a bowl until stiff.

Mix the ground almonds, sugar and the tablespoon of cinnamon together in a separate bowl, then fold through the egg whites.

Wet your hands, roll the mixture into balls, gently flatten them with the palm of your hand and place 2.5cm apart on the lined baking trays. Bake for 18–20 minutes until lightly golden.

Mix the icing sugar and remaining teaspoon of cinnamon together on a plate and spread out, then turn the balls in the mixture while they are still warm, getting them really well coated all over. Leave to cool completely, then turn them again in the spiced sugar and serve.

This is possibly the only recipe in the book that involves anything technical and a few items of kit, as well as arm power, but the end result is worth it. It's a real showstopper of a dessert and the flecks of black halva studded through the white ice cream are a visual delight and a taste sensation. No churning is called for, but you do need to stay close by for some stirring every now and then. Prepare the halva at least 24–36 hours ahead of making the ice cream.

Black Halva and White Chocolate Ice Cream

Serves 6

For the black halva
vegetable or other flavourless oil, for oiling
150g clear honey
200g tahini
3 teaspoons nigella seeds, finely ground
pinch of sea salt

For the ice cream
300ml milk
1 vanilla pod or 1 teaspoon vanilla bean paste
4 egg yolks
30g caster sugar
200g white chocolate, finely chopped
200ml double cream

For the halva, start by lining a 450g loaf tin (around 800ml in capacity) with enough oiled clingfilm to hang over the sides.

Place the honey in a saucepan and heat until it reaches a temperature of 120°C on the sugar thermometer, at which point a drop of honey should form a ball that can be squashed after being dropped into cold water.

Heat the tahini in a separate saucepan until it reaches a temperature of 50°C on the thermometer.

Add the tahini to the honey and whisk together for around 8 minutes until the mixture has thickened and come together. Add the ground nigella seeds and salt, stir well and then pour it into the lined tin. Leave to cool at room temperature before placing in the fridge for 24–36 hours.

For the ice cream, heat the milk and vanilla together in a saucepan to just below boiling point. Whisk the egg yolks and sugar together in a bowl, then very slowly pour a little of the hot milk mixture on top while whisking constantly. Continue adding the remainder of the hot milk mixture until it is all incorporated and then return the mixture to the pan and place over a medium heat. Cook, stirring constantly, for around 10 minutes until the sauce has thickened into a light custard consistency. Remove and discard the vanilla pod, if using.

Add the white chocolate and stir until it has melted, then cover the surface of the custard with clingfilm to prevent a skin forming and leave to cool.

Take the now-set halva and chop into small pieces.

Whisk the double cream in a bowl until soft peaks form, then fold through the cooled custard. Add the chopped halva pieces, place in a freezerproof container that has a lid, cover with the lid and freeze. Stir the ice cream at 30-minute intervals for around 3 hours, then leave to freeze completely. It's best served within a few days, if it lasts that long!

Tip
You will have more halva than you need for this recipe, so store what's left in an airtight container in the fridge; it will keep for up to 3 weeks.

This cake is so simple, yet so tasty. It came about during an apple season when I was trying to be more imaginative with ways to use our generous crop. The lovely texture of the crumble on top of the soft cinnamon-infused cake is a real delight and even better when served warm with a generous scoop of vanilla ice cream.

Apple Crumble Cake

Serves 8

50g unsalted butter, plus extra for greasing
100ml milk
1 large egg
170g plain flour
½ teaspoon table salt
2 teaspoons baking powder
1 teaspoon ground cinnamon
80g caster sugar
2 apples, peeled, cored and finely chopped

For the crumble
2 tablespoons plain flour
4 tablespoons soft dark brown sugar
40g cold unsalted butter, diced
1 teaspoon ground cinnamon

Preheat the oven to 200°C/180°C fan/Gas Mark 6. Grease and line the base of a 20cm round cake tin with baking parchment.

Melt the butter in a saucepan, then add the milk and the egg and whisk together until combined.

Sift all the dry ingredients into a bowl, pour the wet mixture on top and fold to combine, then stir through the chopped apples until they are well incorporated. Pour the cake mixture into the prepared tin.

Place all the ingredients for the crumble in a small bowl and mix together with a table knife (I find using fingers makes the butter too soft and harder to work with). Spread the crumble evenly over the top of the cake mixture and bake for 30 minutes until a skewer inserted into the centre comes out clean, checking every now and then to ensure that the top doesn't get too brown and covering with a sheet of baking parchment if necessary.

Leave the cake to cool in the baking tin for 10 minutes before removing. Serve warm.

Far less challenging than you might think to make, this renowned loaf holds a very powerful significance in Jewish culture and tradition. Two loaves are made for Friday night in commemoration of the Israelites who were exiled from Egypt and as a reminder that God will provide as long as Jews refrain from working on the Sabbath. Traditionally, a prayer for the challah is spoken before the bread is torn and a piece given to each person around the table. In my house, thick slices of the bread are then cut and dunked into Chicken Soup (*see* page 66), or smothered in Chopped Liver (*see* page 63) and Egg and Onion (*see* page 62). I make two loaves simply because the kids love it so much, and it makes a lovely French toast for a weekend treat (*see* page 206).

Challah

Makes 2 loaves

600g white bread flour, plus extra for dusting
4 egg yolks
80ml vegetable oil, plus extra for oiling
90g caster sugar
1 tablespoon fast-action dried yeast
½ teaspoon table salt
270ml water

For the glaze
1 egg, beaten
2 tablespoons sesame seeds (optional)

Put all the ingredients for the challah (except the glaze) in a large bowl and bring everything together with your hands until you have formed a dough. Alternatively, you could use the dough setting on your bread machine if you have one.

Turn the dough out on to a floured board and knead for 5 minutes until it is smooth and elastic. Place in a large, lightly oiled bowl, cover with a clean tea towel or clingfilm and leave in a warm place to rise to double the size; this should take 1½ hours.

Remove the dough from the bowl and divide into 6 equal portions. Roll 3 of the pieces into long ropes around 45cm each and join them together at the top, then plait the pieces to the end and join again at the bottom. Repeat with the remaining 3 pieces of dough to make a second loaf.

Place the 2 loaves on a baking tray lined with baking parchment, re-cover and again leave to rise in a warm, draught-free place for 30 minutes more. Meanwhile, preheat the oven to 170°C/150°C fan/Gas Mark 3½.

Brush the challah with the beaten egg to glaze and sprinkle with the sesame seeds, if you like, then bake for 30–35 minutes until golden brown and the base of the bread sounds hollow when tapped. Leave to cool on a wire rack.

Note
Cholla or challah – however you choose to spell it, the 'c' is always silent.

It was a very rare occurrence but sometimes my family would find ourselves with leftover challah. Now we always make sure we have extra so that the kids can enjoy challah French toast, a firm favourite at the breakfast table on a Sunday morning.

Challah French Toast with Sour Cherry Jam and Whipped Vanilla Mascarpone

Serves 4

3 eggs
85ml milk
2 tablespoons date syrup
1 teaspoon vanilla extract, plus
½ teaspoon for the cream
4 large, thick slices of Challah
(*see page 204*)
1 tablespoon sunflower oil
15g butter
80g mascarpone cheese
80ml double cream
2 tablespoons sour cherry jam
1 tablespoon icing sugar, for dusting

Beat the eggs, milk, date syrup and the 1 teaspoon of vanilla together in a shallow bowl large enough to fit the challah slices in a single layer.

Add the challah slices and leave to soak for 5 minutes, turning them over a few times.

Heat the oil and the butter in a large frying pan until it is sizzling. Fry the challah over a medium heat for 2–3 minutes on each side until golden.

Meanwhile, whisk the mascarpone, cream and remaining ½ teaspoon of vanilla together in a bowl with an electric whisk until soft peaks form.

Place the challah on a plate and top with some of the sour cherry jam and a generous dollop of the mascarpone cream. Dust over the icing sugar and serve.

I love flourless cakes. They taste light and make me feel slightly virtuous eating them. Dates, nuts and chocolate are three of my favourite ingredients, so what better idea than to design a cake recipe where they make the perfect match?

Chocolate, Date and Pistachio Cake

Serves 8

vegetable or other flavourless oil or butter, for oiling/greasing

100g caster sugar

4 eggs, 2 of them separated

75g ground almonds

20g cocoa powder

120g dates, pitted and finely chopped

100g unsalted pistachio nuts, finely chopped, plus extra to decorate

200g dark chocolate, minimum 70% cocoa solids, finely chopped, or chocolate chips

Preheat the oven to 180°C/160°C fan/Gas Mark 4 and oil/grease and line a 450g loaf tin (around 800ml in capacity) with baking parchment.

Whisk the sugar, the 2 whole eggs and 2 egg yolks together in a stand mixer fitted with the whisk attachment or in a bowl with an electric whisk until pale, thick and fluffy; this will take around 10 minutes.

Meanwhile, mix the ground almonds, cocoa powder, dates, pistachios and chocolate together in a large bowl. Fold this almond mixture through the sugar and egg mixture, ensuring that everything is well combined.

Clean out the mixer bowl or whisking bowl and add the 2 egg whites, then whisk until they are stiff. Fold gently through the cake mixture.

Add the cake mixture to the prepared loaf tin and bake for 40–45 minutes or until a skewer inserted into the centre of the cake comes out clean.

Leave the cake to cool in the tin for 10 minutes and then remove and scatter with chopped pistachios. Cut into thick slices to serve.

These truffles came about during *MasterChef* when I needed to find a third date recipe to join my date brûlée and baklava with date syrup. The brief was to make it 'thick, brown and sticky' and I took that brief literally. Given the time constraint – two hours to make three puddings – I thought these dark, sticky gems would work well. Adding Amaretto elevates the truffles to an indulgent treat.

Date, Pecan and Amaretto Truffles

Makes about 15 truffles

100g dates, pitted

75g pecan halves

50g cocoa powder

2 tablespoons Amaretto

1 tablespoon coconut oil

25g desiccated coconut

Place the dates in a food processor and pulse a few times to break them down. Add the pecans and cocoa powder and blend to combine. Then add the Amaretto and oil and blend again until the mixture comes together.

Sprinkle the desiccated coconut on to a plate. Take a heaped teaspoonful of the mixture and roll into a ball, then roll the ball in the coconut. Repeat with the remaining mixture.

Pop the balls into petit four cases and store in an airtight container in a cool, dark place until ready to serve. They will keep for up to 2 weeks.

Kosher laws prohibit the mixing of milk and meat, which means that you either have to get creative and think of dairy-free (*pareve*) desserts to serve after a meat meal, or serve a fish or vegetarian main. While it's hard to beat a classic banoffee pie – with a biscuit base, of course, not pastry – this stands up really well as a great pareve substitute without suffering any hardship. This is more of an assembly job than any serious cooking, but you do need to start the prep the night before you plan to serve by placing the can of coconut milk in the fridge so that you have a creamy consistency for whipping.

Tahini Banoffee Sundae

Serves 4

100g walnut halves
1 tablespoon sesame seeds
100g caster sugar
400ml can coconut milk, chilled overnight in the fridge
2 tablespoons icing sugar
½ teaspoon vanilla extract
200g tahini
75g clear honey
4 bananas

Preheat the oven to 180°C/160°C fan/Gas Mark 4.

Spread the walnuts and sesame seeds out on a baking tray and roast in the oven for 8–10 minutes.

Meanwhile, place the caster sugar in a dry saucepan over a medium heat and wait for it turn a deep amber colour – don't stir, otherwise the sugar will crystallize.

When the caramel is ready, add the roasted nuts and seeds and stir quickly to combine, then tip out on to a silicone baking mat or a sheet of foil and leave until cool enough to handle.

Break the caramel into chunks, add to a food processor and pulse until you have coarse crumbs; don't overwork, as you want to retain some texture. Set aside.

Open the can of coconut milk and add only the firm solids from the top of the can to the bowl of your stand mixer fitted with the whisk attachment, or a large bowl, along with the icing sugar and vanilla. Whisk the ingredients together, with an electric whisk if you don't have a stand mixer, until you have a stiff consistency; this will take about 5 minutes.

Whisk the tahini and honey together in a bowl to combine.

To assemble, start by adding some slices of banana to the bases of 4 short, straight-sided glasses or glass dessert bowls. Top with a spoonful of the tahini mixture, followed by the coconut mixture and then the nut crumble. Repeat the layering – you should get at least 2 layers in each glass – making sure you finish with a very generous sprinkling of nut crumble.

Tip

You can make the nut crumble ahead of time as well as the tahini and honey paste, but the coconut cream will need to be whisked just before serving and the bananas sliced at the last minute to avoid discolouring.

As a woman of little patience, I have never been that enthusiastic about making bread. It's the waiting for it to rise that I find a bit tedious. I do, however, take enormous pleasure in making this sweet Polish bread stuffed full of chocolate and butter, which works so well in this pudding with its double whammy of chocolate. While shop-brought chocolate brioche could serve the same purpose, I would advocate trying homemade; the sense of satisfaction alone makes it so worthwhile. This is an ideal make-ahead dessert, as it positively benefits from sitting in the fridge for up to two days before cooking. I've offered quantities to make two loaves in one go so that you get more for the effort involved – use one for the pudding and freeze the other for later use, if you can resist the temptation to scoff it straight from the oven.

Chocolate Babka Bread and Butter Pudding

Serves 8–10

For the bread
170ml milk
170g caster sugar, plus 2 teaspoons
3 teaspoons fast-action dried yeast
420g plain flour, plus extra for dusting
2 large eggs
1 large egg yolk
1 teaspoon almond extract
½ teaspoon table salt
175g unsalted butter, softened, plus extra for greasing

For the chocolate filling
30g unsalted butter, softened
225g dark chocolate chips
2 tablespoons caster sugar
1 egg, beaten

For the chocolate custard
175g dark chocolate, minimum 70% cocoa solids, broken into pieces, or use chocolate chips
75g caster sugar
400ml double cream, plus extra to serve
60g unsalted butter
3 large eggs
2 tablespoons cocoa powder

Start by making the bread. Heat the milk in a small saucepan or in the microwave – you want it warm but not hot. Add the milk to the bowl of a stand mixer fitted with a paddle attachment with the 2 teaspoons of sugar and sprinkle over the yeast. Leave the mixture to sit for around 5 minutes until it is frothy. If it doesn't froth, you need to start the process again, as the bread dough won't rise properly.

Add 4 tablespoons of the flour to the yeast mixture and mix on a medium speed until it is all combined. Add the whole eggs, egg yolk, almond extract, salt and remaining 170g sugar and continue to beat until everything is incorporated. Reduce the speed to low and gradually add the remaining flour, a tablespoon at a time. Increase the speed again and start adding the butter, a thumb-sized piece at a time, allowing each piece to be fully incorporated before adding the next one.

The dough will now be nice and shiny and very sticky – don't be alarmed at this stage, as it will come together nicely! Scrape the sticky mixture into a lightly greased bowl large enough to allow the dough to rise to double the size. Cover with clingfilm and leave in a warm place to rise; this can take up to 2 hours.

Line 2 × 900g loaf tins (each around 1.5-litre in capacity) with 2 sheets of baking parchment, one running crossways and one lengthways, or use ready-made loaf tin liners. Halve the risen dough and place one half on a well-floured surface (return the other half to the bowl and re-cover with clingfilm). Using a floured rolling pin, roll the dough into a rectangle measuring 46 × 25cm. With a long side nearest to you and leaving a 2.5cm border all the way round, spread half the butter for the filling over the dough, then sprinkle half the chocolate chips and sugar evenly over the top. Brush the border with beaten egg and, starting from the long side furthest away from you, roll the dough into a tight log shape. Bring either end of the log together and then pinch them together to ensure that they are well sealed. Carefully twist the ring twice to make a double figure-of-eight and place in one of the lined loaf tins. Repeat with the remaining half of the dough and filling to make the second loaf.

Cover both loaf tins with greased clingfilm and leave in a warm place to rise to double the size; again, this can take up to 2 hours. Meanwhile, preheat the oven to 180°C/160°C fan/Gas Mark 4.

Once risen, brush both the loaves with the remaining beaten egg and bake for around 30–40 minutes until golden brown and the base of the bread sounds hollow when tapped. Remove the loaves from the tins and leave to cool completely on a wire rack.

At this point, you can wrap one of the loaves up in a double layer of clingfilm and foil and freeze for later use; it will keep for up to a month.

For the pudding, grease a 2-litre baking dish. Cut the cooled bread into slices, then cut each slice diagonally in half to make triangles. Set aside.

To make the custard, put the chocolate, sugar, cream and butter in a glass bowl and either set over a saucepan of simmering water, ensuring that the base of the bowl doesn't touch the water, or heat in the microwave in 30-second bursts, until everything has melted together.

In a separate bowl, whisk the eggs until light and fluffy and then pour the melted chocolate mixture over the top and add the cocoa powder. Give the mixture another whisk, then pour about one-third of the custard into the baking dish. Add the triangles of bread, layering as you go, until the whole dish is covered. Pour the remaining custard over the top, ensuring that all the pieces of bread are coated. Lightly press the top of the bread with a fork so that it is fully immersed in the custard, then cover with clingfilm and place in the fridge for a minimum of 2 hours but anything up to 2 days is great.

When you are ready to cook, preheat the oven to 200°C/180°C fan/Gas Mark 6. Bake, uncovered, for 30 minutes until the top is crunchy and golden. Remove from the oven and leave to sit for around 10 minutes before serving with a generous dollop of double cream.

My mother-in-law fondly recalls enjoying this as a hot drink in the markets of Jerusalem on cold winter nights. Getting her thumbs-up for this recipe was very important to me before I could present it to the *MasterChef* judges, and although I knew it would divide the crowd, I was prepared to take the risk to bring something new and different to the table. It's traditionally known as *sahlab*, the name for a flour made from the tubers of an orchid, and depending on which part of the Middle East you are from, it's either enjoyed hot as a winter warmer or cold as a dessert. This is a lovely sweet pudding, fragrant with rosewater and cinnamon, and best enjoyed cold when it's nice and thick with a generous sprinkling of toasted nuts and coconuts.

Almond and Rosewater Rice Pudding

Serves 6

50g ground rice
3 tablespoons cornflour
1.2 litres milk
75g caster sugar
1 tablespoon rosewater
50g ground almonds
50g desiccated coconut
2 tablespoons flaked almonds
25g unsalted pistachio nuts
3 tablespoons date syrup

To decorate
ground cinnamon
large handful of edible dried rose petals (optional)

Mix the ground rice and cornflour with enough of the milk to make a paste. Place the remaining milk in a saucepan over a low heat and bring gently to the boil. Add the sugar and simmer gently for 2–3 minutes. Gradually add the ground rice and cornflour paste, stirring constantly with a wooden spoon to avoid it catching on the base of the pan, and simmer over a very gentle heat for around 10–15 minutes or until the mixture is nice and thick.

Add the rosewater a teaspoon at a time and check for flavour; it can be overpowering, so add to taste. Stir in half the ground almonds and simmer for another few minutes.

Turn off the heat and leave the mixture to cool for around 10 minutes.

While the rice pudding is cooling, heat a dry frying pan over a medium heat, add the coconut and toast for a few minutes, then set aside. Toast the flaked almonds in the same pan. Cut the pistachios into slithers or lightly crush them, then set aside.

Divide the rice pudding between 6 glasses, filling each one around three-quarters full. Top with a drizzle of date syrup, a generous pinch of the toasted coconut, the remaining ground almonds and the pistachios, then sprinkle with the toasted flaked almonds, some cinnamon and the edible rose petals if you like.

For me, sticky toffee pudding was always the ultimate dessert to choose on a menu. Rich and gooey with melting vanilla ice cream on top, I can fondly recall scraping every last drop of the thick brown sauce from my spoon, always wanting a few bites more. These slightly pimped-up, generously sized individual puddings are a real crowd-pleaser, particularly in the cold winter months when a dessert has to be hot, sticky and very comforting. Serve with a large dollop of good-quality vanilla ice cream or some double cream.

Cherry Sticky Toffee Puddings with Caramelized Pecans and Tangerine Sauce

Serves 6

75g unsalted butter, softened, plus extra for greasing
200g dried cherries
150ml boiling water
2 tablespoons Cointreau or other orange-flavoured liqueur of your choice
½ teaspoon bicarbonate of soda
150g golden caster sugar
2 eggs, beaten
175g self-raising flour

For the caramelized pecans
50g butter
100g pecan halves
50g soft dark brown sugar

For the sauce
175g light muscovado sugar
125g unsalted butter
6 tablespoons double cream
25g pecan halves, chopped
juice of 1 tangerine

Preheat the oven to 180°C/160°C fan/Gas Mark 4.

Lightly grease 6 individual metal pudding basins or ramekins, then line the base of each with a circle of greaseproof paper.

Put 175g of the dried cherries into a bowl and pour over the measured boiling water. Stir in the liqueur and bicarbonate of soda, then leave to sit for an hour.

Beat the butter and golden caster sugar together in a large bowl until pale and fluffy, then slowly beat in the eggs a little at a time. Add the cherry mixture, then the flour and fold in with a large metal spoon.

Divide the mixture equally between the prepared basins or ramekins, place on a baking tray and bake for around 25 minutes until well risen and firm.

Leave the puddings to cool in the basins or dishes while you prepare the nuts and the sauce.

For the caramelized pecans, melt the butter in a saucepan over a medium heat, then add the pecans and stir well to coat. Add the brown sugar and stir until the nuts have caramelized. Turn out on to a sheet of baking parchment and leave to cool and harden.

To make the sauce, put the muscovado sugar, butter, cream, pecans and remaining cherries in a saucepan and heat gently until the sugar has dissolved, then stir in the tangerine juice.

Turn each pudding out on to a plate and top with the sauce and the caramelized pecans.

Variation

You can replace the cherries with any other dried fruit of your choice.

This is one of my favourite showstopping desserts. The crunchiness of the pastry against the light frangipane filling along with the soft fruit is a winning combination, plus the colours make this as pleasing on the eye as it is on the palate. Ripe apricots are my first choice of stone fruit here, but white peaches also work really well when in season. *Mahleb* (also known as *mahlepi*, among other variants) powder is produced by grinding the seed kernels from the stones of the St Lucie cherry, and has a bitter almond-cherry flavour.

Apricot and Orange Blossom Frangipane with Pistachios

Serves 8–10

For the pastry
175g plain flour, plus extra for dusting
1 teaspoon mahleb (mahlepi) powder
pinch of table salt
175g cold unsalted butter, cut into cubes
50g icing sugar
2 egg yolks

For the frangipane
175g unsalted butter, softened, plus extra for greasing
175g caster sugar
175g whole blanched almonds
2 eggs
1 tablespoon orange blossom water
6 ripe apricots, halved and stoned
15g unsalted pistachio nuts, chopped

Place the flour, mahleb powder, salt and butter in a food processor and pulse to combine. Add the icing sugar and egg yolks and pulse until the mixture starts to come together into a dough.

Turn out on to a lightly floured work surface, gather into a ball and then wrap in clingfilm and refrigerate for an hour.

Grease a 23cm loose-bottomed tart tin. Grate the pastry dough coarsely into the tart tin, making sure that the base and sides are evenly covered and there are no gaps. Return to the fridge for a further 30 minutes. Meanwhile, preheat the oven to 200°C/180°C fan/Gas Mark 6.

Line the pastry case with a sheet of baking parchment and fill with baking beans or rice, then bake blind for 15 minutes. Carefully remove the paper with the beans or rice (some of the pastry may separate, so gently press back together with the back of a spoon) and bake, uncovered, for a further 10 minutes until lightly golden. Leave the pastry case to cool completely while you make the filling. Reduce the oven temperature to 170°C/150°C fan/Gas Mark 3½.

Beat the softened butter and sugar together in a stand mixer fitted with the paddle attachment or in a bowl with a wooden spoon until pale and light.

Add the almonds to a food processor and pulse to a coarse rubble; you don't want powder, so be careful not to overwork them. Beat the almonds into the butter and sugar, then beat in the eggs, one at a time, and finally add the orange blossom water, mixing until everything is combined.

Spoon the frangipane mixture into the pastry case and top with the apricot halves, cut-side up. Bake for 50 minutes. Remove from the oven and sprinkle with the chopped pistachios, then bake for a further 20 minutes.

Leave the tart to cool in the tin completely before removing and slicing.

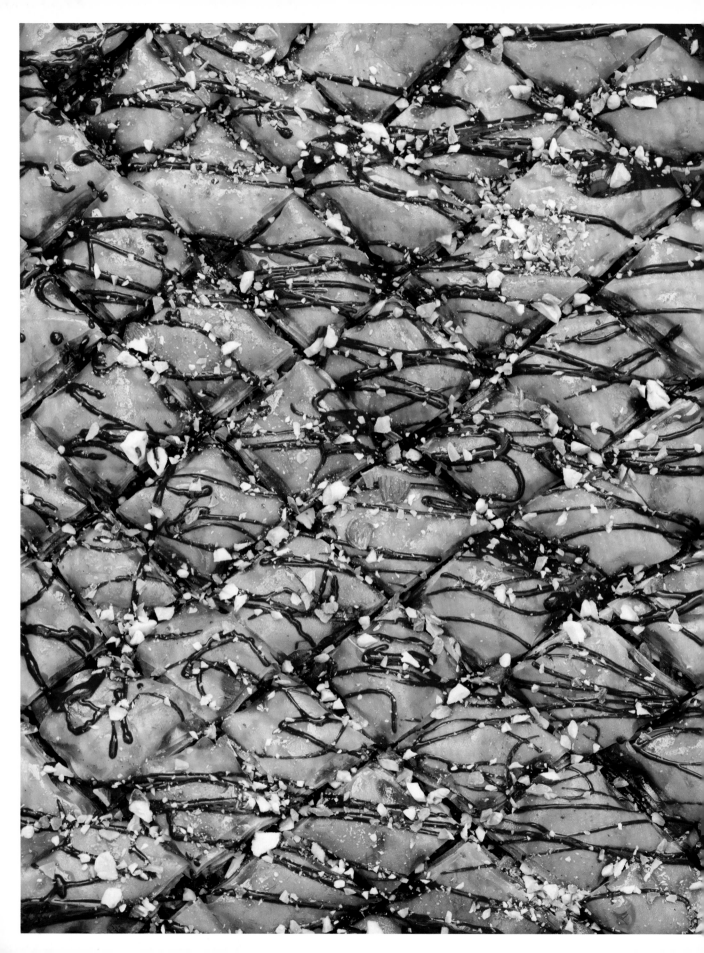

Baklava is the ultimate Middle Eastern treat with all the key attributes: sweetness, stickiness and nuttiness. My version of these little delicacies, contains a few more spices (of course) and a drizzle of chocolate at the end (why not?) just to give it that extra hit of sugar.

Baklava with Chocolate Drizzle

Makes 24 generous pieces

For the baklava
200g pecan halves
100g unsalted pistachio nuts, plus extra to decorate
100g whole unblanched almonds
125g unsalted butter
1 teaspoon vanilla bean paste
75g soft dark brown sugar
½ teaspoon ground cardamom
1 teaspoon ground mixed spice
1 teaspoon ground cinnamon
pinch of freshly grated nutmeg
2 x 270g packets of filo pastry sheets
100g dark chocolate chips, melted, to decorate

For the syrup
175ml water
125g granulated sugar
50g date syrup
1 teaspoon vanilla bean paste
1 cinnamon stick

Preheat the oven to 190°C/170°C fan/Gas Mark 5.

Spread all the nuts out on a large baking tray, about 28 × 19cm, and toast in the oven for 10 minutes.

Meanwhile, melt the butter in a small saucepan over a low heat.

When the nuts are ready, tip into a food processor and pulse until finely chopped but still with some coarse bits. Alternatively, chop the nuts by hand. Add the vanilla bean paste and give one final mix. Transfer the nut mixture to a bowl, add the sugar and spices and mix together thoroughly.

Grease the 28 × 19cm baking tray with some of the melted butter and cut the filo sheets to fit. The best way to avoid pastry wastage is to place your tray vertically on one half of the pastry sheet, and if it is roughly half, you can cut straight down the middle to give you double the sheets.

Add the first sheet of pastry to the tray and liberally brush it with the melted butter using a pastry brush, then repeat 6 times. Sprinkle a generous layer of nuts on top, then splash some melted butter over the nuts with the brush to help the first sheet of pastry stick to the nuts. Repeat the layering using another 4 filo sheets, spreading each sheet with more melted butter each time. Add another layer of nuts before finishing with the final 6 sheets, then give the top sheet a good coating of melted butter.

Place the tray in the fridge for 30 minutes, or up to 24 hours if making ahead.

Put all the ingredients for the syrup in a saucepan, stir and bring to a rolling boil over a medium heat, then reduce the heat and simmer for 10 minutes, stirring often, until thickened.

When ready to bake, preheat the oven to 180°C/160°C fan/Gas Mark 4.

Remove the baklava from the fridge. Set the pan horizontally and cut across the baklava from left to right in a series of diagonal lines spaced about 3cm apart, then repeat in the other direction. Bake for 20–25 minutes, rotating the pan halfway through to ensure that the top browns evenly.

Remove the baklava from the oven and immediately pour the syrup over the top, discarding the cinnamon stick, making sure that you coat all the pieces evenly. If you have the time (and the willpower), leave the baklava to sit and cool completely so that the syrup can fully soak in.

Drizzle with the melted chocolate and scatter with chopped pistachios.

Natalie Allen, the lovely owner of the Sweet Things bakery in Primrose Hill and Notting Hill Gate in London, was kind enough to share this delicious recipe with me. Make sure you use really good-quality dark chocolate, as you need that lovely rich, slightly bitter flavour to counteract the sweetness.

Chocolate Fondant Cake

Serves 8–10

cocoa powder, for dusting

200g good-quality dark chocolate, minimum 70% cocoa solids, broken into pieces

200g salted butter, plus extra for greasing (or use vegetable oil)

160g caster sugar

5 eggs

1 tablespoon plain flour (gluten-free is fine)

To serve
vanilla ice cream
raspberries

Preheat the oven to 190°C/170°C fan/Gas Mark 5.

Grease a 20cm springform cake tin with butter or oil and dust with cocoa powder; you won't need to line the tin if you do this thoroughly enough.

Put the chocolate and butter together in a glass bowl and either set over a saucepan of simmering water, ensuring that the base of the bowl doesn't touch the water, or heat in the microwave in 30-second bursts, until melted.

Stir in the sugar, then add the eggs, one at a time, beating in each one with a wooden spoon before adding the next. Add the flour and mix well, then transfer to the prepared tin.

Bake for 20–25 minutes; the cake should still tremble in the middle. Leave to cool completely in the tin, then serve at room temperature, or serve chilled with some vanilla ice cream and raspberries.

My mum's rum chocolate mousse was legendary. I think this recipe was adapted from an Evelyn Rose cookbook that she loved, but whether the famous Jewish cook herself used quite as much rum as Mum is something we will never know. The absence of dairy (if using kosher chocolate) makes it a great pareve dessert. Use dark chocolate only for a kosher option; it will just be a little richer.

Rum Chocolate Mousse

Serves 8

200g dark chocolate, minimum 70% cocoa solids, broken into pieces

150g milk chocolate, broken into pieces (*see above*)

2 tablespoons dark rum

8 eggs, separated

Put the chocolate with the rum in a glass bowl and either set over a saucepan of simmering water, ensuring that the base of the bowl doesn't touch the water, or heat in the microwave in 30-second bursts, until melted. Leave the melted chocolate mixture to cool a little, then gradually stir in the egg yolks.

Whisk the egg whites in a separate large bowl until stiff, then gently fold through the chocolate mixture.

Pour the mousse into a bowl of your choice, cover with clingfilm and leave to set in the fridge for a minimum of 6 hours.

The recipe for this cake came from the lovely students at Les Roches Royal Academy of Culinary Arts in Jordan where I was fortunate enough to enjoy a meal cooked by them. I love all things simple when they taste this good. There is no need to use fancy olive oil, but the flavour is more robust if you use a stronger-flavoured one like extra virgin. Just a few simple raspberries or strawberries on top are all it needs to shine.

Olive Oil Cake

Serves 10–12

180g caster sugar
2 large egg yolks
2 tablespoons fresh lemon juice
grated zest of ½ lemon
110g plain flour
160ml olive oil, plus extra for oiling
3 egg whites
pinch of table salt
raspberries and strawberries, to serve

Preheat the oven to 180°C/160°C fan/Gas Mark 4. Oil and line the base of a 23cm loose-bottomed cake tin.

Place 120g of the sugar, the egg yolks and lemon juice and zest into the bowl of a stand mixer fitted with a paddle attachment and beat together for 5 minutes, scraping down the sides once or twice, or use a bowl and a wooden spoon if making by hand. Slowly add the flour and mix for 2 minutes, then drizzle in the olive oil and continue to beat until it is well combined and glossy. Transfer the cake mixture to a bowl and clean out the mixer bowl. Replace the paddle attachment with the whisk attachment, or use an electric whisk and a clean bowl.

Add the egg whites and salt to the mixer bowl and whisk until stiff. Slowly add the remaining 60g sugar and continue to whisk until the mixture forms stiff peaks.

Fold the egg white mixture into the cake mixture in 3 stages until it is all combined. Add to the prepared tin and bake for 25–30 minutes or until a skewer inserted into the centre of the cake comes out clean. Leave to cool completely in the tin, but don't be alarmed if it starts to crack as it cools; it's all part of the charm.

Sprinkle raspberries and strawberries on top before serving.

Matzo is traditionally eaten over Passover when the consumption of leavened products containing the five forbidden grains – wheat, barley, oats, rye and spelt, known as *chametz* – is forbidden. Store cupboards become stuffed full of these delicious crackers and the quest begins to try and be as creative as possible with them for the eight days of the 'feast without the yeast'. We tend to eat matzo all year round, simply because this eggy breakfast delicacy with a generous sprinkle of cinnamon sugar is the kids' absolute favourite weekend breakfast, and even better that it's Daddy wearing the apron for a change.

Carl's Matzo Brei

Serves 2

3 large matzo squares
175ml boiling water
2 eggs, beaten
¼ teaspoon table salt
15g unsalted butter
½ teaspoon ground cinnamon
3 teaspoons granulated sugar

Break the matzo sheets into roughly 2.5cm pieces or, better still, get the kids to do it. Add to a bowl and pour over the measured boiling water. Give it a stir, then cover with a plate or clingfilm and leave for 5 minutes until the matzo pieces have softened.

Add the eggs and salt and mix until everything is combined.

Melt the butter in a frying pan over a medium heat, add the matzo mixture and flatten down with a spatula to make a large pancake. Cook for 3 minutes, then check if the underside is golden and use the spatula to cut the pancake into quarters. Turn the pieces over and cook for a further 3–4 minutes until golden brown. Remove the matzo brei to a plate.

Mix the cinnamon and sugar together, then sprinkle over the top of the matzo brei. Eat straight away.

Arabic desserts are always very sweet, heavily laden as they are with sugar syrup, and this cake is no exception. It is, however, so moist and tasty that you can almost momentarily forget about the calorie content. I slightly adapted this recipe from the wonderful Abbey Road restaurant, run by Chef Hani, in Madaba, Jordan.

Semolina and Coconut 'Harese' Cake

Serves around 15

250g fine semolina
250g desiccated coconut
225g caster sugar
1 heaped teaspoon baking powder
500g full-fat natural yogurt
175ml corn oil
50g unsalted butter, melted
2 tablespoons light tahini

For the sugar syrup
350g caster sugar
175ml water

Preheat the oven to 220°C/200°C fan/Gas Mark 7.

First make the sugar syrup. Put the sugar and measured water into a saucepan, bring to the boil and cook for 10 minutes over a medium heat until the sugar has dissolved and the mixture has slightly thickened. Leave to cool while you make the cake.

Mix all the ingredients except the tahini together in a large bowl, stirring well to make sure that everything is properly combined.

Using a pastry brush, spread the tahini over the base of a 32 × 24cm baking tray, add the cake mixture and spread it out evenly.

Bake for 18 minutes until the top is springy and lightly golden. Leave the cake to cool in the tin for 10 minutes, then pour the sugar syrup evenly over the top. Leave the cake to cool completely before cutting into generous squares.

This beloved classic Jewish pudding is a cross between a crème brûlée and a cheesecake in taste and consistency. A real departure from the stodgy and rather bland noodle kugel I grew up eating, I apologize in advance to those I offend with its much-needed makeover.

Sweet Noodle Kugel

Serves 10–12

1 Earl Grey tea bag
150ml boiling water
150g sultanas
300g dried egg noodles (I like Manischewitz from the kosher section)
60g butter, plus extra for greasing
4 eggs
250g ricotta cheese
400g full-fat cream cheese
150g caster sugar
2 tablespoons ground cinnamon
grated zest of 1 orange
2 teaspoons orange blossom water

For the brûlée topping
6 tablespoons demerara sugar
1 tablespoon sesame seeds

Preheat the oven to 200°C/180°C fan/Gas Mark 6 and lightly grease a 32 × 24cm baking dish.

Place the tea bag in a bowl, pour over the measured boiling water and leave to brew for 2–3 minutes, then add the sultanas. Cover and leave for as long as possible, up to 24 hours, but ideally at least an hour.

Cook the noodles in a saucepan of salted boiling water according to the packet instructions until tender. Drain, add the butter and fork through.

Beat the eggs and cheeses together in a bowl with a wooden spoon, or use a stand mixer fitted with the paddle attachment, until smooth. Discard the tea bag and add the sultanas with their soaking liquid to the cheese mixture, along with the caster sugar, cinnamon, orange zest and orange blossom water. Add the noodles and give everything a good mix to combine, then place in the greased dish and bake for 30 minutes until set.

For the brûlée topping, preheat the grill to its highest setting. Mix the demerara sugar with the sesame seeds and scatter over the top of the cooked kugel, then pop the kugel under the grill until the sugar is golden and bubbling. This is best eaten hot, but it's also delicious cold.

My mother-in-law fondly recalls her mother making ma'amoul biscuits when she was a little girl, the filling of lightly spiced dates oozing out of the centres of their very light, crumbly shells. Having enjoyed these biscuits myself across the Middle East, I wanted to do justice to my mother-in-law's memory. These are traditionally made using a beautiful wooden ma'amoul mould (available on Amazon or eBay for less than £10). While it's not essential to the taste, it is to their delightful appearance, so I would strongly urge you to buy one.

Spiced Date 'Ma'amoul' Biscuits

Makes 45 biscuits

¼ teaspoon fast-action dried yeast

55ml tepid water

225g unsalted butter, at room temperature

40ml vegetable oil, plus extra for oiling the mould if using

80g icing sugar, plus extra for dusting

½ teaspoon orange blossom water

1 teaspoon vanilla extract

pinch of table salt

1 heaped teaspoon mahleb (mahlepi) powder

500g plain flour, sifted

For the date filling

200g pitted Medjool dates

½ teaspoon vegetable oil

1 teaspoon ground cinnamon

½ teaspoon ground allspice

½ teaspoon ground nutmeg

¼ teaspoon ground ginger

Preheat the oven to 180°C/160°C fan/Gas Mark 4. Line 2 large baking trays with baking parchment.

Add the yeast to a bowl, pour over the measured tepid water and mix together. Leave to sit for 5 minutes.

Beat the butter and oil together in a stand mixer fitted with the paddle attachment for around 3 minutes until well combined, or use a large bowl and a wooden spoon if making by hand. Add the icing sugar and continue to beat until it is incorporated, then add the yeast mixture, orange blossom water and vanilla extract and continue to beat on a slow speed. With the machine running, add the salt and mahleb powder, then add the flour, bit by bit, until it is combined. Continue to beat for another minute, then transfer the dough to a bowl and leave to rest for 15 minutes while you make the date filling.

Roughly chop the dates, add to a food processor with the oil and process until you have a thick paste, or finely chop if you don't have a food processor. Add the spices and mix them in well.

Take a walnut-sized amount of the dough, roll it into a ball and then form it into a bowl by turning it around and using your thumb and forefinger to make a hole wide enough to add the filling. Place a teaspoonful of the filling in the hole, then bring the top of the dough over the filling to cover it and reshape into a ball. Lightly oil your mould, if using, and add the ball, pressing it into the shape. To remove the biscuit from the mould, hold it by the handle, turn it over and tap it on to a wooden board. Continue with the remaining dough, placing the biscuits on the lined trays about 1cm apart.

If you don't have a mould, proceed as above by rolling the dough into balls, filling and sealing, but press down on the top of the balls with the tines of a fork to make a pretty pattern.

Bake the biscuits for 15–18 minutes, rotating the trays halfway through if necessary, until very pale gold in colour; take care not to overcook.

Leave the biscuits to cool on the tray for 5 minutes before transferring to a wire rack and then dusting liberally with icing sugar.

This tart celebrates the combination of orange and chocolate beautifully. Rich and indulgent, it makes a killer dinner party dessert for which your guests, no matter how full they may be, will always find room.

Dark Chocolate and Orange Tart

Serves 8–10

For the pastry
340g plain flour, plus extra for dusting
100g icing sugar
30g cocoa powder
200g cold unsalted butter, cut into cubes, plus extra for greasing
grated zest of 1 orange
1 egg
pinch of table salt

For the filling
300ml whipping cream
230g dark chocolate, minimum 70% cocoa solids, finely chopped
2 tablespoons Cointreau or other orange-flavoured liqueur of your choice
grated zest of ½ orange

To decorate
grated zest of ½ orange
cocoa powder

If you have a food processor, add all the ingredients for the pastry to it and pulse until the mixture just comes together in a ball. If making by hand, sift the flour, icing sugar and cocoa powder together into a bowl, and then, using your fingertips, gently work the butter into the flour mixture until it resembles breadcrumbs. Mix in the orange zest, then finally add the egg, beaten, and salt and gently work everything together until you have a ball of dough.

Dust the pastry with a little flour, then gently press down on the ball of dough to flatten into a round. Wrap in clingfilm and leave to rest in the fridge for 30 minutes.

Preheat the oven to 200°C/180°C fan/Gas Mark 6 and lightly grease a 23cm tart tin.

Roll the pastry out between 2 sheets of greaseproof paper or clingfilm, rotating the pastry after each rolling, until it is around 5mm thick. Remove the top sheet of paper or clingfilm and carefully roll the pastry around your rolling pin, then unroll over your tart tin. Gently press the pastry into the sides of the tin and remove the top layer of paper or clingfilm. Trim off the excess pastry with a knife, or roll your rolling pin over the top, then prick the base all over with a fork and return to the fridge for a further 30 minutes.

Take a sheet of greaseproof paper, scrunch it into a ball and then unwrap it and use it to line your pastry case. Fill the case with baking beans or rice and bake blind for 15 minutes. Carefully remove the paper with the beans or rice and bake, uncovered, for a further 6–8 minutes until golden. Leave the tart case to cool completely.

For the filling, bring the cream to a simmer in a saucepan. Remove from the heat, add the chocolate and stir into the cream to melt, then add the liqueur and orange zest and continue stirring until the mixture is smooth.

Pour the chocolate mixture into the cooled tart case, and then leave in the fridge to set for a minimum of 3 hours, covered loosely with foil, ensuring that the foil doesn't touch the top of the tart. Decorate with grated orange zest and a dusting of cocoa powder.

Tip

This tart benefits from being served with something a little sharp to offset the richness, so some berries or unsweetened crème fraîche would work well.

My husband's late grandmother Celia, better known to my kids as Ggma, fled from Vienna in 1938, taking her deep-rooted Austrian values and cherished family recipes with her. Her famous apple strudel is her greatest legacy. I never managed to do it justice when I tried to reconstruct it, so I've replaced the fiddly filo with a light pastry. If you are using a tart variety of apple like Bramley, you will need to add sugar to the filling, but if you have opted for a dessert apple such as Granny Smith, you can leave sugar out of the filling altogether.

I think Ggma would like my version, but I can still imagine her telling me off in her thick German accent for changing hers.

Viennese Apple Turnover

Serves 8

beaten egg white, to glaze

2 tablespoons flaked almonds, for sprinkling

double cream, vanilla ice cream or custard to serve (optional)

For the pastry

600g plain flour, plus extra for dusting

400g cold unsalted butter, cut into cubes

200g icing sugar, plus 2 tablespoons for dusting

5 large egg yolks, beaten

For the filling

1.5kg cooking apples, such as Bramley, or dessert apples, such as Granny Smith, peeled, cored and chopped into 2cm pieces

40g raisins

2 tablespoons ground cinnamon, plus 1 teaspoon for dusting

1 teaspoon ground mixed spice

50g caster sugar (or more or less depending on the type of apple used)

If you have a food processor, add all the ingredients for the pastry to it and pulse until the mixture just comes together in a ball. If making by hand, add the flour to a bowl, and then, using your fingertips, gently work the butter into the flour until the mixture resembles breadcrumbs. Mix in the sugar, then add the egg yolks and work everything together until you have a ball of dough. Wrap in clingfilm and chill in the fridge for 30 minutes.

Preheat the oven to 200°C/180°C fan/Gas Mark 6.

Divide the pastry into a 60:40 ratio, as you want a bit more pastry for the top, then rewrap the larger piece and return to the fridge. Using a rolling pin lightly dusted with flour, roll the smaller piece into a large rectangle about 2cm thick on a sheet of baking parchment; don't worry about making it too uniform, as you will be shaping it later. Transfer to a baking tray and bake, uncovered, for 5 minutes. Remove from the oven and leave to cool.

For the filling, mix the apples, raisins and spices together in a bowl, then sprinkle over the sugar. Pile the filling on top of the pastry, leaving a 1cm border around the edge. Roll out the remaining pastry on a lightly floured work surface so that it is large enough to cover the filling. Brush the egg white around the border of the base layer of pastry and lay the larger sheet over the top, making sure that the apple filling is well covered and that the 2 pieces of pastry join. Cut around the edges with a sharp knife to make a neat rectangle and press down with a fork to make a pretty pattern and help ensure that none of the juice from the filling escapes). Using a sharp knife, cut 2 or 3 holes in the top to allow the steam to escape. Glaze the top with beaten egg white and sprinkle over the flaked almonds. If you have time, pop the tray in the fridge for 30 minutes.

Bake the turnover for 45 minutes–1 hour until the top is golden brown. Leave to cool slightly before mixing the remaining 2 tablespoons icing sugar and cinnamon together and dusting liberally over the top.

Slice and serve with some double cream, vanilla ice cream or custard, if liked.

Index

Acknowledgements

There are a few people I would like to thank for their support, encouragement and belief in me.

First, my incredible husband and girls, the driving force behind everything I do. Even though I made you all eat a lot, pretty much every day for six months, you always appreciated it (even when some experiments went horribly wrong) and praised me (knowing that criticizing wasn't an option). Carl, you are my rock, and although I may not tell you enough, I couldn't do what I do without you.

To my agent Heather Holden-Brown at HHB Agency who totally got me at our first-ever meeting. She said there was a book in me and here I am. I would also like to thank Alison Starling and her amazing team at Octopus for their support, guidance and, more importantly, for giving me this opportunity. Juliette Norsworthy and Leanne Bryan, you were both so lovely to work with. Rosie Reynolds, Clare Winfield and Linda Berlin; you are geniuses with your styling and photography.

To my mum Hilary and sisters Debbie and Samantha for their support and encouragement. My childhood memories of food and mealtimes are always remembered fondly, even when they included tears and tantrums in restaurants for there not being enough food! To my in-laws, particularly Judith and her siblings for their family recipes, and to all extended family members who helped out in many other ways; Ros and Doug, you know who you are!

To my *MasterChef* family, who nurtured me and calmed my nerves through the most stressful experience I have ever known.

To the Jordan Tourist Board and Tara Gandhi at Brighter PR who helped me to put together such an incredible experience in my quest to feed my obsession with Middle Eastern food. And now for all the people on the ground who welcomed me into their beautiful country, homes, kitchens and restaurants: thank you to Hashem Restaurant, Habibah Sweets and the RACA (Royal Academy of Culinary Arts) in Amman, Um Amer, Um Hamza, Captain's Desert Camp in Wadi Rum, chef Mohammed Asmar at the Mövenpick Tala Bay in Aqaba, Al Qantarah Restaurant in Petra and lastly (but not least) Issam Hirzallah and Haneen Karadsheh for looking after us so well and being such lovely company; your passion and love of your beautiful country knows no limits.

To Helen Graham for your recipe contributions. You are a wonderful, talented chef with killer recipe ideas and a bright future ahead of you, and I loved our experimental foodie sessions in my kitchen.

Thank you also to a very talented lady I met over Instagram, @mandyliciouschallah, for her foolproof challah recipe.

To all my recipe testers: Debbie, Laura, Jo, Julien and Emma.

To Staub and Zwilling, my culinary partners, for their *crème de la crème* of cookware and knives; cooking is a lot more pleasurable when you have top-notch equipment. To Beloved Dates for the endless supply of your Date Nectar date syrup (I got through bucket-loads), Providence Deli, Al Arz Tahini (it's seriously the best I have ever tasted), the incredible shop Pulia in Borough Market (Georges, you are a star), Mark at South West Garlic Farm for your supply of black garlic and to Walter Purkis and Sons, my local fishmongers – how lucky I am to have you round the corner.

I also want to thank my late father Bernie. I didn't tell him enough how special and incredibly influential he was in my life. It's only now that I am married with kids of my own that I can see just how exceptional a father he was. I know how proud he would have been of this book.

Author biography

Emma Spitzer was born and raised in Brighton, southern England, to Jewish parents of Polish and Russian descent.

Her love of cooking started at a very early age. Emma shadowed her mother in the kitchen as she regularly cooked traditional Ashkenazi Jewish dishes passed down from her Polish parents. Emma now loves to draw influences from her travels through the Middle East, her cultural heritage and her mother-in-law's North African roots. She creates food with lots of passion and lots of spice. Her style is big, bold flavours with many different ingredients coming together on one plate.

Emma's ambition started at an early age; at 28 she set up a travel business selling luxury spa holidays across the world. In 2007 the company launched its award-winning second brand, Tots Too, which offers luxury family holidays worldwide.

Following her success on reaching the final of BBC 1's *MasterChef*, Emma has been in high demand. She has been teaching cookery classes and demonstrating at food festivals, running sell-out supper clubs and catering for private dining events. She lives in north London with her husband, four young daughters and their cat.